PLANT-BASED SIMPLE

Quarto.com

First Published in 2025 by Fair Winds Press, an imprint
of The Quarto Group, 100 Cummings Center, Suite 265-D,
Beverly, MA 01915, USA.
T (978) 282-9590 F (978) 283-2742

Fair Winds Press titles are also available at discount for
retail, wholesale, promotional, and bulk purchase. For details,
contact the Special Sales Manager by email at specialsales@
quarto.com or by mail at The Quarto Group, Attn: Special
Sales Manager, 100 Cummings Center, Suite 265-D,
Beverly, MA 01915, USA.

29 28 27 26 25   1 2 3 4 5

ISBN: 978-0-7603-9653-7

Digital edition published in 2025
eISBN: 978-0-7603-9654-4

Library of Congress Cataloging-in-Publication Data is
available.

The content in this book was previously published in *Epic
Vegan Quick and Easy* by Dustin Harder (Fair Winds Press,
2021), *Vegan Bowl Attack!* by Jackie Sobon (Fair Winds Press,
2016), *Vegan Yack Attack's Plant-Based Meal Prep* by Jackie
Sobon (Fair Winds Press, 2020), and *Great Gluten-Free Vegan
Eats* by Allyson Kramer (Fair Winds Press, 2012).

Photography: Jackie Sobon on pages 4, 19, 23, 25, 33, 34, 37,
38, 57, 61, 62, 67, 83, 87, 89, 109, 120, 127, 128, 130, 148, 168,
170, 173, 179, 180, 182, 185, 194, 196, 198, 211, 229, and 231;
Ashley Madden from riseshinecook.ca, @riseshinecook, on
pages 7, 9, 13, 15, 43, 47, 48, 53, 77, 80, 103, 111, 115, 118, 159,
162, 207, and 226; Allyson Kramer on pages 69, 73, 74, 92,
95, 97, 98, 133, 136, 139, 141, 143, 144, 147, 151, 177, 187, 188,
190, 193, 204, 214, 217, 218, 220, 223, 225, 232, and 235

Design and page layout: Kelley Galbreath

Printed in China

PLANT-BASED SIMPLE

150 DELICIOUS WHOLE-FOOD, NUTRIENT-DENSE RECIPES *for* HEALTHY LIVING

RECIPES BY
Dustin Harder, Jackie Sobon, and Allyson Kramer

FAIR WINDS

Contents

Introduction

When you first go vegan, you might be tempted to survive on "healthy" frozen meals and take-out. But costs will more than likely start adding up, and you may quickly decide to get into cooking your own delicious vegan food.

It's time to get comfortable in your kitchen. Experiment with the recipes, playing around with ingredients you already love and ones that might be new to you. Soon, you will be quietly introducing your friends to veganism with the aid of the perfect soup.

After all, you will have some great conversations about veganism with people and some not-so-great ones, too. But nothing makes a believer out of people more than putting a beautiful and delicious dish in front of them that does not have any animal products in it.

When you hear, "Wow! This is so good!" your response can be, "Right? Can you believe that I don't eat just grass and dirt all day?" (Just kidding. Only say this to someone you know really well.) Then you can start bringing vegan cookies or appetizers to gatherings of friends and family. Many people just don't realize how awesome and fun cruelty-free food can be.

And that's exactly where this book comes into play! It offers a wide variety of recipes for every palate preference, whether you are into comfort food, eating light, trying out new flavors, or just in need of something delicious and satiating. Invite some of your close ones over and chow down on recipes that won't disappoint!

CHAPTER ONE

Breakfasts

All-in-One Breakfast Sheet-Pan Bowls

YIELD: 4 SERVINGS

Nothing is better to me than a well-seasoned tofu scramble and some crispy breakfast potatoes! Make both at the same time with this one sheet-pan recipe. In thirty-five minutes you'll have breakfast ready for the family without missing Saturday morning cartoons.

4 cups (310 g) frozen hash browns, shredded

Cooking spray

1½ teaspoons sea salt, divided

½ teaspoon black pepper

½ teaspoon Old Bay Seasoning

1 package (14 ounces [396 g]) extra-firm tofu, drained and crumbled

¼ cup (20 g) nutritional yeast

½ teaspoon ground turmeric

½ teaspoon Himalayan black salt (kala namak) (optional)

1 red bell pepper, roughly chopped

½ red onion, thinly sliced

1 cup (70 g) sliced baby bella or white button mushrooms

2 cups (60 g) spinach, chopped

4 scallions, thinly sliced (optional)

Preheat the oven to 415°F (213°C, or gas mark 7). Line a large sheet pan with parchment paper.

Add the potatoes to the sheet pan and spread in one layer. Spray with cooking spray and sprinkle with 1 teaspoon salt, pepper, and Old Bay. Toss until all the potatoes are coated, place in the oven, and bake for 10 minutes.

Remove the sheet pan from the oven, flip the potatoes, and move over to the left side of the sheet pan. Spray the sheet pan with cooking spray and add the tofu to the right of the potatoes. Sprinkle the tofu with the remaining ½ teaspoon salt, nutritional yeast, turmeric, and black salt (if using). Toss the tofu until the spices are evenly dispersed and push tofu to the center of the pan. Add the vegetables to the right of the scramble and spray everything with cooking spray.

Return to the oven and bake for 10 minutes. Flip everything and bake for 10 minutes, until the tofu has crisped slightly on the top, potatoes have darkened, and vegetables have shrunk slightly in size.

Remove the sheet pan from the oven and immediately sprinkle the spinach over the top of everything. Use a spatula to mix the spinach in until well dispersed, mixing everything together and wilting the spinach as it mixes in.

Divide the mixture among 4 bowls and garnish with scallions (if using). See tip to make the bowl epic.

Note

Create your epic with this dish by adding vegan sausage, sliced avocado, a drizzle of sriracha, and a sprinkle of everything-bagel seasoning.

Skillet Bagel Breakfast Sandwiches for Two

YIELD: 2 SANDWICHES

Beloved breakfast elements on a soft and chewy bagel with toasty crispy outsides—it's a win! Pick breakfast sausage patties that are the size of the bagel you plan to use. Don't be shy to add items you love to this sandwich, such as avocado or everything-bagel seasoning. You can even swap the veggies out in the quick scramble.

2 vegan breakfast sausage patties

1 tablespoon (15 ml) olive oil

¼ cup (30 g) diced onion

½ cup (122 g) extra-firm tofu, drained and crumbled

¼ teaspoon ground turmeric

¼ teaspoon garlic powder

¼ teaspoon Himalayan black salt (kala namak) (optional)

¼ cup (45 g) chopped tomato

½ cup (15 g) baby spinach

2 slices vegan cheese of choice

1 tablespoon (15 ml) water

2 large vegan bagels of choice, toasted (see Note)

Sriracha or ketchup (optional)

Prepare the breakfast sausages according to package directions and set aside.

In a medium skillet with a fitted lid, heat the oil over medium-low heat. Add the onion and sauté for 3 minutes, until soft. Add the tofu, turmeric, garlic powder, and black salt (if using). Mix with a spatula, until everything is combined and the tofu has turned light yellow. Cook for 3 minutes, until everything is heated throughout.

Add the tomato and spinach to the skillet. Mix with a spatula until everything is well combined and the spinach has wilted. Move the tofu mixture to one side of the skillet and place the sausage patties in the clearing. Divide the tofu mixture on top of each patty. Move the patties with tofu to the center of the skillet and place a slice of cheese on each mound.

Have the lid to the skillet ready in hand and add the tablespoon of water to the skillet. Cover immediately to create steam. Leave covered 40 to 60 seconds, until the cheese melts completely. Uncover and transfer the patty-tofu-cheese-covered mounds to each bottom bagel half. Drizzle with sriracha or ketchup (if using). Cover with the top half of the bagel and serve warm.

Note

Use butter to go the extra step and get the restaurant-quality touch. Either butter the bagel when it comes out of the toaster, or butter it before you toast it face down in a hot skillet until browned and crispy.

Maple Balsamic Brussels Sprouts and Sweet Potato Hash

YIELD: 6 TO 8 SERVINGS

Back in the days before I went vegan, I tried every diet imaginable. The point-counting system was in that mix. I'll never forget these sweet and tangy Brussels I had once from the point-counting company's recipe bank. I took it a step further here and paired crunchy and savory Brussels with sweet, tasty, and delicately textured sweet potatoes. Mix in spices, oil, and vinegar to bring this perfectly sweet and savory breakfast side dish to life. But hey, add some kale to the mix for a banging lunch that will make your coworkers jealous. Breakfast is really an all-day affair in my eyes anyway.

2 medium sweet potatoes, peeled and cut into ½-inch (1 cm) cubes

2 tablespoons (30 ml) olive oil, divided

3 cups (270 g) Brussels sprouts, trimmed and roughly chopped

1 teaspoon garlic powder

½ teaspoon sea salt

¼ teaspoon black pepper

2 tablespoons (40 g) maple syrup

1 tablespoon (15 ml) balsamic vinegar

Fresh thyme (optional)

Preheat the oven to 415°F (213°C, or gas mark 7). Line a large sheet pan with parchment paper.

Add the potatoes to the prepared sheet pan, drizzle with 1 tablespoon (15 ml) of olive oil, and toss to coat all pieces. Bake for 15 minutes. Remove from the oven and add the Brussels. Sprinkle with garlic powder, salt, and pepper. Drizzle with the remaining olive oil and the maple syrup. Toss with a spatula to evenly coat the pieces.

Bake for 20 minutes, until the pieces of sweet potato and Brussels start to brown and are fork-tender. Remove from the oven, drizzle with balsamic, and toss to coat. Transfer to a serving dish and garnish with thyme (if using).

Baked French Toast Sticks

As a kid, I always begged to have the frozen French toast sticks in the freezer. I can't recall us having them all too often. Maybe because I gobbled them up so fast! I love this version because I can make ahead and freeze them. They also don't have all the nonsense ingredients store-bought ones have. Baked in the oven, these are crispy, cinnamony, sweet, and savory delicious bites for adults and kids. Served with some premium maple syrup on the side, it's an excellent breakfast for any day of the week.

PLANT-BASED SIMPLE

¼ cup (32 g) flax meal

½ cup (120 ml) water

½ vegan baguette cut into 12 sticks

¼ cup (60 g) unsweetened applesauce

2 tablespoons (14 g) ground cinnamon

3 tablespoons (36 g) organic cane sugar

¼ teaspoon sea salt

1 tablespoon (15 ml) vanilla extract

Cooking spray

Maple syrup

Preheat the oven to 350°F (180°C, or gas mark 4). Line a sheet pan with parchment paper.

In a bowl, combine the flax meal and water. Set aside to thicken for 5 minutes. While it thickens, cut the bread into 1-inch (2.5 cm)-thick and 4-inch (10 cm)-long pieces, 12 sticks total. A baguette works best.

Add the applesauce, cinnamon, sugar, salt, vanilla, and the flax mixture to a large bowl. Mix until combined.

Spray the sheet pan generously with cooking spray. Dip the bread sticks into the mixture, quickly coating on all sides but not submerging. Avoid making the sticks soggy with the mixture. Transfer to the prepared sheet pan and continue dipping bread sticks until all are coated.

Bake for 15 minutes. Gently slide the spatula under each stick completely and flip each one. Bake for 15 minutes, until dark brown and crispy. Serve warm with maple syrup.

Note

These can also be made ahead and frozen—yup, just like the ones you used to get at the grocery store! After baking, let them cool completely and transfer to an airtight container or resealable plastic bag. Store in the freezer for up to 4 months. To reheat in the microwave, simply arrange on a microwave-safe plate and heat for 30 to 60 seconds, until heated through. To reheat in the oven, arrange on a parchment paper-lined sheet pan and bake at 350°F (180°C, or gas mark 4) for 12 minutes, or until warmed through.

Sweet and Savory Scones

YIELD: 12 SCONES

Scones are upgraded biscuits full of limitless possibilities. This recipe offers just two options, but I urge you to mix in your own favorite ingredients once you master these two. Some of my other favorites include pumpkin, cranberry, brown sugar, pecan, triple berry, vegan bacon, cheddar, and garlic. Don't be scared. Try your favorite ingredients and play with your food once you get the hang of this recipe! For those who like a little spice, take the optional add-in of jalapeño in the sausage cheddar scones to kick up the heat.

FOR THE SCONE DOUGH

½ cup (120 ml) unsweetened plain almond or soy milk, plus more for brushing

1 tablespoon (15 ml) apple cider vinegar

2 cups (250 g) all-purpose or gluten-free all-purpose flour

¼ cup (50 g) organic cane sugar

1 tablespoon (14 g) baking powder

½ teaspoon sea salt

6 tablespoons (84 g) cold vegan butter, cut or spooned into chunks

FOR THE LEMON RASPBERRY SCONES

1 cup (150 g) frozen or fresh raspberries

1 tablespoon (15 ml) lemon extract

1 tablespoon (13 g) organic cane sugar (optional)

Lemon zest (optional)

FOR THE SAUSAGE CHEDDAR SCONES

2 vegan sausages, roughly chopped

1 cup (115 g) vegan cheddar shreds

1 jalapeño, seeded and minced (optional)

Preheat the oven to 350°F (180°C, or gas mark 4). Line a large sheet pan with parchment paper. In a bowl, whisk together the milk and vinegar. Set aside to thicken for 5 minutes.

To make the scone dough
Add the flour, sugar, baking powder, and salt to a bowl and whisk until well combined. Add the butter and use a fork, dough cutter, butter knife, or fingers to cut the butter into the flour mixture until the texture has become like sand. Add in the milk and mix with a spatula or wooden spoon until well combined. Do not overmix.

To make the lemon raspberry scones
Fold in the raspberries, lemon extract, sugar, and zest (if using).

To make the sausage cheddar scones
Fold in the sausage, cheddar shreds, and jalapeño (if using).

Scoop the batter out in ¼-cup (60 ml) portions onto the prepared sheet pan. Bake for 10 minutes, remove from the oven, and brush the tops with milk. Rotate the sheet pan in the oven and bake for 18 to 20 minutes, until cooked through and the bottoms are golden brown.

Note

Use a food processor to quickly cut the butter into the flour mixture. Add the flour, sugar, baking powder, salt, and butter to a food processor. Pulse until a sand consistency is reached. Transfer the mixture to a bowl and follow the directions as written.

Presto Pesto Avocado Toast

YIELD: 2 SERVINGS

Avocado toast is where it's at, am I right? Avocado and toast is fine, truly. You can smash an avocado up on dry toast and it will be delightful. But why not take a few minutes and spruce up that dried toast! With just a few simple ingredients your toast goes from "yass" to "ohhhh YASSSSS" in minutes. Skip the pesto if you want and use a drizzle of truffle oil, freshly cracked pepper, and edible flowers for a colorful bite for brunch. See the tip for a bonus avocado toast that is my all-time favorite!

FOR THE PESTO

1 cup (40 g) packed fresh basil leaves

½ cup (60 g) walnuts

⅓ cup (79 ml) olive oil or vegetable broth for oil-free

2 tablespoons (28 ml) water

1 clove garlic

2 tablespoons (10 g) nutritional yeast

1 tablespoon (16 g) white miso

Juice of ½ lemon

½ teaspoon sea salt

FOR THE AVOCADO TOAST

1 avocado, peeled and diced

Juice of ½ lemon

Sea salt (optional)

Black pepper (optional)

2 pieces vegan bread, toasted

Crushed red pepper

To make the pesto

Add all the ingredients to a blender. Blend until there are still some specks of basil visible. Some people like the specks; others like smooth and creamy. Go whichever route you prefer, blending a little longer to make it smooth and creamy, if you desire.

To make the avocado toast

Add the avocado and lemon juice to a bowl. Mash with a fork just until well combined. There should still be chunks of avocado. Season with salt and pepper to taste (if using).

Divide the avocado mixture atop the 2 pieces of toast, spreading it out evenly on each piece. Drizzle each piece of toast with the desired amount of pesto, and sprinkle with crushed red pepper. Serve immediately.

Note

My all-time favorite quick fix with avocado toast is the lemon avocado mixture at left, topped with a generous drizzle of sriracha and a hefty sprinkling of everything-bagel seasoning. I'm not sure you will ever eat it any other way after you try this! But I encourage you to try both ways mentioned on this page and pick your favorite.

Cheap 'n Cheesy Jalapeño Grits

YIELD: 6 SERVINGS

The combo of melted cheese and spicy jalapeños is always a win for people who like spice. You can't see me, but I'm raising my hand. I'm always looking for ways to house the perfect pair, and creamy grits are the best vehicle for these two. This is easy to make in one pot and a great addition to any brunch spread.

2 tablespoons (28 g) vegan butter or canola oil

2 jalapeños, seeded and diced (see Note)

2 cloves garlic, minced

2 cups (475 ml) plain unsweetened soy or almond milk

2 cups (475 ml) water

1 teaspoon sea salt, plus more to taste

1 cup (140 g) uncooked yellow grits, polenta, or yellow stone-ground cornmeal

1 cup (80 g) nutritional yeast

1 cup (115 g) vegan cheddar shreds, plus more for garnish

Fresh sliced jalapeños or pickled jalapeños from a jar (optional)

Black pepper, to taste

Add the butter to a medium saucepan and melt over medium-low heat. Add the jalapeños and sauté for 2 to 4 minutes, until soft. Add the garlic and sauté for 1 minute, until fragrant.

Slowly add the milk, water, and salt to the pot. Raise the heat to high and bring to a boil. Lower the heat to a simmer, and add the grits and nutritional yeast. Whisk vigorously for 4 to 6 minutes working the lumps out, until thick and creamy. Add the cheese to the grits and mix with a spoon until well combined.

Season with salt and pepper to taste. Serve warm, sprinkled with shredded vegan cheddar and jalapeños (if using).

Note

When chopping a jalapeño, wear gloves if you have them. If you don't, a plastic baggie over your hand that handles the pepper will do the trick depending on the size of your hand. Some form of protection is always helpful. Handling a jalapeño and taking your contact lenses out later do not mix. Clearly, I know this from an experience a friend had, not myself. Anyway, cut the top off the pepper and slice the pepper in half lengthwise. Use a small spoon or gently use the blade of the knife to scrape the membrane and seeds from the jalapeño's flesh. Dice as needed.

Chai Waffle Stick Dippers

Waffles are a quintessential brunch food that many people love. I always saw waffles as a special weekend meal that I enjoyed far too little. Now, you can take the awesomeness of waffles and turn them into a fun finger food, filled with chai spices and dipped into maple butter. Wins all around!

PLANT-BASED SIMPLE

FOR THE WAFFLE STICKS

¾ cup (175 ml) orange juice

¾ cup (175 ml) unsweetened nondairy, soy-free, nut-free milk

1 tablespoon (15 ml) olive oil

1 teaspoon vanilla extract

1¼ cups (156 g) unbleached all-purpose flour

½ cup (40 g) rolled oats

2 tablespoons (24 g) organic cane sugar

2 teaspoons baking powder

1½ teaspoons ground cinnamon

¾ teaspoon ground ginger

½ teaspoon ground cardamom

½ teaspoon ground allspice

½ teaspoon ground cloves

FOR THE MAPLE BUTTER DIP

¼ cup (55 g) soy-free vegan butter, melted

⅓ cup (80 ml) maple syrup

¼ teaspoon ground cinnamon

To make the waffle sticks
Place all the waffle ingredients in a blender and puree until combined and smooth. Let the mixture thicken for 10 minutes.

Preheat a Belgian waffle maker according to the manufacturer's instructions. Fill with batter and cook for 10 minutes or until the steam stops coming out (if you have a newer waffle maker, the light turns green). Repeat until the batter is used up. If you like, keep the cooked waffles warm at a low temperature in the oven while you make the remaining ones.

To make the maple butter dip
While the waffles are cooking, whisk the butter, maple syrup, and cinnamon together in a bowl and then separate the dip among 4 small bowls for serving.

When the waffles are done, cut them into strips with a serrated knife and serve with the dip.

Apple Pie Smoothie Bowls

For many people, apples mean that fall and cooler temperatures have arrived, and although the former may be the case in Southern California, temperatures still remain warm into November. With this apple pie smoothie bowl, you can celebrate the change of seasons while keeping your cool.

FOR THE APPLE PIE SMOOTHIE

1½ pounds (680 g) green apples, cored and chopped

2 frozen bananas, peeled

3 cups (90 g) packed fresh spinach

1 teaspoon ground cinnamon

1 teaspoon vanilla extract

Pinch of salt

2 teaspoons maca powder (optional)

Unsweetened nondairy soy-free milk (optional)

FOR THE PIE TOPPING

¼ cup (36 g) raw almonds

¼ cup (45 g) dried dates, pitted

¼ teaspoon ground cinnamon

Pinch of salt

To make the apple pie smoothie
Place all the ingredients in a blender in the order listed. Press the apple pieces down firmly in the pitcher, as they will create the liquid needed to puree the rest of the ingredients. Blend until very smooth. If you would like a thinner consistency, add some soy-free nondairy milk. Pour into 2 bowls and store in the freezer while making the topping.

To make the pie topping
In a food processor, pulse the almonds, dates, cinnamon, and salt together until they are small chunks. Shake over the top of each smoothie bowl and serve.

Peanut Butter Pretzel Oatmeal

YIELD: 2 SERVINGS

Who else has a hard time passing by the peanut butter pretzel bins in the bulk section of the grocery store without wanting to buy bags of them? It can't only be me. The salty, crunchy snacks are a welcome addition to this breakfast of creamy oats.

1 cup (235 ml) unsweetened soy-free nondairy milk

⅓ cup (80 ml) water

¼ cup (65 g) peanut butter

3 tablespoons (45 ml) maple syrup

1 teaspoon vanilla extract

⅔ cup (53 g) rolled oats

Pinch of salt

½ cup (30 g) peanut butter pretzels, broken into smaller pieces

Maple syrup, for serving (optional)

In a small pot, combine the soy-free nondairy milk, water, peanut butter, maple syrup, vanilla, and rolled oats over medium heat. Bring to a boil, adjust the heat to medium-low, and simmer for 5 minutes, stirring occasionally, until the oats are fully cooked.

Stir in the salt and divide the oatmeal between 2 bowls, topping each with ¼ cup (15 g) of crushed peanut butter pretzels and a light drizzle of maple syrup, if using.

Baked Berry Oatmeal

YIELD: 5 SERVINGS

Even though traditional oatmeal comes together quickly, baked oatmeal has a special place in my heart. I love the "set it and forget it" aspect of this recipe, as you just dump everything into one dish, stir it around, and leave it in the oven to take care of itself.

1½ cups (360 ml) warm water

2 tablespoons (17 g) chia seeds

2½ cups (230 g) rolled oats

4 cups (600 g) mixed berries (strawberries, blueberries, etc.), cut into bite-size pieces if necessary, divided

⅔ cup (66 g) raw walnut halves or sunflower seeds, divided

1 cup (235 ml) plain unsweetened nondairy milk

⅓ cup (80 ml) maple syrup or agave nectar

2 teaspoons vanilla extract

¼ teaspoon salt

Preheat the oven to 350°F (180°C, or gas mark 4). Mix the water and the chia seeds in a large liquid measuring cup and set aside. Place the oats, half of the berries, and half of the walnuts in a 9-inch (23 cm) round baking dish.

Add the nondairy milk, maple syrup, vanilla, and salt to the chia mixture and whisk until well combined. Pour the mixture into the baking dish and gently stir to incorporate. Bake the oatmeal for 45 minutes, until slightly golden in color. The oatmeal should be a little soft, as it will firm slightly while cooling. Let the oatmeal cool on a rack for 20 minutes. Cut it into fifths, place in 5 storage containers, and top each serving with the remaining berries and walnuts. Oatmeal can be stored in the refrigerator for up to 7 days or in the freezer for up to 3 months.

Note

In a pinch, frozen berries work well here. They may get a little soggy in the topping, but they'll still taste good.

Matcha Oatmeal

YIELD: 4 SERVINGS

Oatmeal has always been a favorite breakfast of mine because it is so easy to customize and comes together in minutes! Here I've added a little matcha powder for a light caffeine kick and wonderful flavor. The sweetness of the oatmeal goes perfectly with tart raspberries!

3 ½ cups (830 ml) water

3 cups (323 g) rolled oats

1 cup (235 ml) plain unsweetened nondairy milk, divided

⅓ cup (80 ml) agave nectar

2 teaspoons (10 ml) vanilla extract

2 teaspoons (6 g) culinary matcha powder

⅛ teaspoon salt

1 cup (125 g) fresh raspberries

¼ cup (20 g) unsweetened coconut flakes

½ teaspoon black sesame seeds

In a large pot over medium heat, bring the water, oats, and ¾ cup (175 ml) of the nondairy milk to a boil. Adjust the heat to medium-low and simmer, stirring occasionally, until the oats start to break down and become creamy, 5 to 7 minutes. While the oats are cooking, whisk together the remaining nondairy milk, agave nectar, vanilla, and matcha powder in a small ramekin or bowl until there are no clumps.

Add the matcha mixture and the salt to the oatmeal, stirring until combined. When the oatmeal has thickened to your liking, divide it between 4 bowls or storage containers, then top with raspberries, coconut flakes, and sesame seeds. Serve while warm or store in the refrigerator for up to 7 days.

Sesame Apricot Granola

YIELD: 6 SERVINGS

This recipe started off as a bit of a fluke some time ago, and it has now become my favorite granola! Tahini does a great job of clumping the grains, seeds, and dried apricots together, and when combined with maple, cardamom, and coconut, it is all taken to the next level of granola greatness.

½ cup (48 g) gluten-free rolled oats

½ cup (30 g) unsweetened large coconut flakes

½ cup (92 g) raw buckwheat groats

½ cup (50 g) raw almonds, chopped

½ cup (26 g) dried apricots, diced

2 tablespoons (30 g) chia seeds

2 tablespoons (16 g) sesame seeds

¼ teaspoon ground cardamom

⅛ teaspoon salt

¼ cup (60 g) tahini

3 to 4 tablespoons (45 to 60 ml) maple syrup, or preferred sweetness

1 teaspoon vanilla extract

Preheat oven to 350°F (180°C, or gas mark 4) and line a baking sheet with a silicone baking mat or parchment paper.

In a large bowl, combine the rolled oats, coconut flakes, buckwheat groats, almonds, apricots, chia seeds, sesame seeds, cardamom, and salt. In a smaller bowl, whisk together the tahini, maple syrup, and vanilla.

Add the wet mixture to the dry mixture and fold together until evenly coated. Spread the granola out over the lined baking sheet and bake for 10 minutes, stirring it around halfway through. Transfer it to a cooling rack for 5 minutes before eating or storing for later. This granola tastes great on plain coconut milk yogurt with a light drizzle of maple syrup or agave nectar.

Melon Madness Bowls

YIELD: 4 SERVINGS

While driving through Los Angeles, you are bound to come across one of the thousands of fresh fruit carts that are parked on various street corners. One of the foods they offer at these carts is a mixed fruit cup with a side of zesty chili powder shake. Improving upon this treat, we have here a flavorful melon breakfast with added spice and wholesome hemp seeds.

1 pound (455 g) honeydew melon, scooped into balls

1 pound (455 g) cantaloupe, scooped into balls

1 pound (455 g) watermelon, scooped into balls

2 tablespoons (28 ml) lime juice

½ teaspoon grated lime zest

½ teaspoon chili powder

¼ teaspoon cayenne pepper

¼ teaspoon salt

¼ cup (37 g) hulled hemp seeds

In a large bowl, toss the honeydew, cantaloupe, and watermelon balls with the lime juice, lime zest, chili powder, cayenne pepper, and salt. Chill in the refrigerator for 30 minutes.

Divide among 4 bowls, sprinkle the hemp seeds over the top of each, and serve.

Nectarine Quinoa Porridge

YIELD: 2 SERVINGS

Comforting porridge does not always have to be made with oats. Instead, try enjoying protein-rich quinoa topped with warm nectarines for a breakfast change-up.

1½ cups (255 g) plus 1 cup (170 g) sliced nectarines, divided

⅔ cup (116 g) quinoa, rinsed and drained

⅔ cup (160 ml) unsweetened nondairy milk

3 tablespoons (27 g) coconut sugar

1½ teaspoons vanilla extract

¼ cup (31 g) roasted shelled pistachios

In a medium pot over medium heat, stir together 1½ cups (255 g) of the nectarines, the quinoa, nondairy milk, coconut sugar, and vanilla, and then bring to a boil. Adjust the heat to medium-low and simmer, partially covered, for 25 minutes or until the quinoa is cooked through, stirring occasionally.

Divide the quinoa between 2 bowls, top each with ½ cup (85 g) of the remaining sliced nectarines and half of the pistachios and serve.

Note

Make this recipe in every season by substituting nectarines with mixed berries in the spring, persimmons in the fall, and cranberries in the winter.

Neapolitan Smoothie Bowls

YIELD: 2 SERVINGS

Who says you can't have ice cream for breakfast? Make this healthy smoothie bowl to get a frosty taste of rich chocolate, creamy vanilla, and tart strawberry layers, topped with fresh fruit and crunchy cacao nibs. You can prep the chocolate and vanilla layers the night before and just finish with the strawberry layer and garnishes in the morning.

FOR THE CHOCOLATE LAYER

1 cup (252 g) frozen banana pieces

3 tablespoons (15 g) raw cacao powder

4 Medjool dates, pitted

Pinch of salt

⅓ cup (80 ml) water

FOR THE VANILLA LAYER

1½ cups (378 g) frozen banana pieces

¼ cup (37 g) hulled hemp seeds

3 Medjool dates, pitted

Seeds scraped from ½ of a vanilla bean

Pinch of salt

⅓ cup (80 ml) water

FOR THE STRAWBERRY LAYER

1½ cups (382 g) frozen strawberries

3 Medjool dates, pitted

½ cup (120 ml) water

1 tablespoon (15 ml) lemon juice

FOR THE FINISHING TOUCHES

½ cup (85 g) sliced fresh strawberries

½ cup (75 g) sliced fresh bananas

2 tablespoons (16 g) cacao nibs

2 tablespoons (18 g) hulled hemp seeds

To make the chocolate layer

Place all the ingredients in a blender and puree until smooth. Divide between 2 bowls and place them in the freezer until set, about 30 minutes.

To make the vanilla layer

Place all the ingredients in a blender and puree until smooth. Divide between the 2 bowls and place them in the freezer until set, about 30 minutes (or overnight if you are prepping the night before).

To make the strawberry layer

Place all the ingredients in a blender and puree until smooth. Divide between the 2 bowls.

Finishing touches

Top each smoothie bowl with sliced strawberries, sliced bananas, cacao nibs, and hemp seeds. Serve immediately.

Note

Soak your dates in warm water for 15 minutes before making this recipe so that they blend more smoothly.

Overnight Chai Chia Pudding

YIELD: 5 SERVINGS

I'm a huge fan of adding caffeinated beverages to my morning meals, and the comforting flavor of chai spice makes it perfect for this chia pudding! While the base is subtly flavored, the diced pears and pecans offer welcome sweetness and crunch.

2 cups (475 ml) boiling water

2 chai tea bags

2½ cups (570 ml) unsweetened almond milk

¼ cup (60 ml) agave nectar

1 teaspoon vanilla extract

Pinch salt

1 cup (163 g) chia seeds

2 pounds (907 g) pears, cored and diced

½ cup (55 g) chopped pecans

In a large liquid measuring cup or bowl, pour the boiling water over the tea bags and steep for 7 to 10 minutes, depending on how strong you prefer the tea flavor to be. Discard the tea bags, squeezing out as much liquid as possible, and whisk the almond milk, agave nectar, vanilla, and salt into the tea. Stir in the chia seeds and divide the loose mixture between 5 jars or airtight containers.

Divide the pears and pecans evenly among the jars. Cover the jars and refrigerate for at least 8 hours or up to 5 days.

Soyrizo Sheet-Pan Hash

YIELD: 5 SERVINGS

Can I admit something here? Sometimes, I am just plain bad at making hash. Clearly, I have an issue with patience, because I can never wait long enough for the potatoes to brown before moving them around. With this sheet pan hash, I don't have to worry about it; plus, it makes way more than you could fit in a single skillet.

1½ pounds (680 g) russet or Yukon Gold potatoes, diced into ¼-inch (6 mm) pieces

6 ounces (170 g) baby bella or cremini mushrooms, stemmed and diced

1 red onion, diced

1 green bell pepper, diced

1 red bell pepper, diced

½ teaspoon dried oregano

1 package (11 ounces [310 g]) soyrizo

1 avocado

1 lime

Preheat the oven to 450°F (230°C, or gas mark 8) and line a baking sheet with parchment paper. In a very large bowl, combine the potatoes, mushrooms, onion, bell peppers, and oregano. Squeeze the soyrizo into the bowl and mix using your clean hands, making sure that the soyrizo evenly coats all the veggies.

Spread the mixture in an even layer on the baking sheet and roast until the potatoes are cooked through, about 50 minutes, stirring halfway through roasting. Move the baking sheet to a rack and let cool for 5 minutes before dividing up between 5 plates or airtight containers. If serving the hash right away, slice the avocado and the lime, divide the avocado evenly among the plates, and garnish each plate with a lime wedge. If storing the hash, slice the avocado and lime just before serving. The hash can be stored in the refrigerator for up to 7 days or in the freezer for up to 3 months.

Note

If you can't find soyrizo in stores near you, try substituting roughly 11 ounces (310 g) of vegan grounds plus 1 tablespoon (15 ml) organic sunflower oil and 2 teaspoons (5 g) chili powder.

Blueberry Smoothie Jars

YIELD: 5 SERVINGS

Smoothie jars make getting out the door during the week so much easier. This recipe is the base version of my favorite—and most commonly made—smoothie, because blueberries and pineapple are so dreamy together. I've ordered the ingredients in the recipe to make the smoothies easy to blend. I like keeping bananas at room temperature so that each morning I can add one to the blender pitcher before dumping the jar contents on top.

2½ cups (265 g) frozen chopped spinach, broken into pieces

4 cups (560 g) frozen blueberries

2½ cups (365 g) frozen pineapple chunks

1 cup (150 g) hemp hearts

1¼ teaspoons ground turmeric

1¼ teaspoons ground ginger

5 small bananas

3¾ cups (890 ml) water

Set out five 24-ounce (710 ml) wide-mouth jars. Divide the spinach, blueberries, pineapple, hemp hearts, turmeric, and ginger evenly among the jars; screw the lids on the jars and store in the freezer.

When you're ready to make a smoothie, add one peeled banana, broken into chunks, to the blender. Run warm water over the outside of one covered jar to help release the frozen ingredients. Pour the jar contents into the blender, followed by ¾ cup (175 ml) water. Blend until completely smooth, then transfer back to the jar and enjoy.

Note

Smoothies are highly customizable, so try this recipe as-is first, then swap in your favorite fruits, spices, or proteins for different versions. During the summer, I like to substitute half of the banana for peach slices.

Minty Peach Yogurt Bowls

YIELD: 5 SERVINGS

Eating yogurt for breakfast seems like a pretty obvious suggestion, but believe me, with a little help from some fresh ingredients it gets so much better! I used peaches and mint here, but another good combination is strawberries and basil.

48 ounces (1,360 g) plain nondairy yogurt

¼ cup (60 ml) maple syrup

3 tablespoons (18 g) minced fresh mint

2 teaspoons (10 ml) vanilla extract

5 cups (405 g) chopped peaches (fresh or thawed frozen)

1 cup (123 g) roasted pistachios

2½ cups (90 g) brown rice crisps cereal

In a medium bowl, stir together the yogurt, maple syrup, mint, and vanilla until combined. Divide the mixture between 5 bowls or jars, then top with peaches and pistachios. Top each bowl with ½ cup (18 g) cereal just before serving. Yogurt bowls can be stored in the refrigerator for up to 5 days.

Chocolate Raspberry Smoothie Jars

YIELD: 4 SERVINGS

Some days I'm craving a bright, tropical smoothie to start my day, but other times, I need something a little richer, and this chocolate raspberry number hits the spot! The little bit of caffeine from the cocoa probably doesn't hurt, either.

3 cups (545 g) frozen raspberries

2 cups (390 g) chopped bananas

1 cup (67 g) firmly packed chopped kale, stems removed

½ cup (70 g) hemp hearts

¼ cup (20 g) cocoa powder

¼ cup (38 g) coconut sugar

Pinch salt

4 cups (960 ml) water

Set out 4 24-ounce (710 ml) wide-mouth jars. Layer ¾ cup (135 g) frozen raspberries, ½ cup (97 g) bananas, and ¼ cup (17 g) kale into each jar. Next, divide the hemp hearts, cocoa powder, coconut sugar, and salt evenly among the jars; screw the lids on and store in the freezer.

When you're ready to make a smoothie, run warm water over the outside of 1 jar to help release the items inside. Pour the jar's contents into a blender, followed by 1 cup (235 ml) water. Blend until completely smooth, then transfer back to the jar and serve.

Note

I love to add a half scoop of my favorite vegan chocolate protein powder to these smoothie jars to give them even richer chocolate flavor!

Avocado Lime Pudding Parfaits

YIELD: 4 SERVINGS

While avocado is good on damn near everything, it's especially versatile in sweet recipes. You've probably seen it used as a sneaky ingredient in chocolate pudding, but I love showing off its green color and brightening its flavor with lime in this breakfast parfait.

2 cups (440 g) mashed avocado

¾ cup (175 ml) plain unsweetened nondairy milk

⅓ cup (80 ml) agave nectar

3 tablespoons (45 ml) lime juice and 2 teaspoons (4 g) zest

Pinch salt

2 cups (290 g) fresh blueberries

½ cup (70 g) raw pumpkin seeds (pepitas)

In a food processor equipped with an S-blade, process the avocado, nondairy milk, agave nectar, lime juice and zest, and salt until completely smooth, scraping down the sides as needed.

Set out 4 jars or storage containers with lids. To layer the parfaits, scoop about ⅓ cup (80 g) pudding into each jar, followed by ¼ cup (38 g) blueberries and 1 tablespoon (10 g) pumpkin seeds. Repeat for a second set of layers, then refrigerate the parfaits until chilled. Parfaits can be stored in the refrigerator for up to 5 days.

Note

While chilling the pudding allows the flavors to really meld together for optimum results, if you're short on time, you can keep all your ingredients in the refrigerator before assembling and forgo the chill time!

Buckwheat Breakfast Bowls

YIELD: 4 SERVINGS

My love affair with buckwheat began only a few years ago, but I'm still sad that it didn't start earlier! This versatile, gluten-free grain is easy to cook, has a wonderfully nutty flavor, and is excellent in this breakfast bowl.

2 cups (475 ml) water

1⅓ cups (228 g) buckwheat groats

1 cup (235 ml) plain unsweetened nondairy milk

¼ cup (60 ml) maple syrup, plus more for optional drizzling

2 tablespoons (10 g) cocoa powder

2 teaspoons (10 ml) vanilla extract

¼ teaspoon ground cinnamon

⅛ teaspoon salt

3 cups (450 g) sliced bananas

¼ cup (65 g) natural almond butter

Bring the water and buckwheat groats to a boil in a large pot. Adjust the heat to medium-low, cover, and simmer stirring occasionally until the groats are tender, 12 to 15 minutes. Adjust the heat to low and stir in the nondairy milk, maple syrup, cocoa powder, vanilla, cinnamon, and salt. Adjust seasoning and consistency as desired (the buckwheat should be of a porridge consistency).

Divide the buckwheat between 4 bowls or storage containers and top with bananas, almond butter, and a little drizzle of maple syrup, if using. Serve warm or store in the refrigerator for up to 7 days.

Hash Brown–Crusted Frittata

YIELD: 4 SERVINGS

While I do love a good omelet, sometimes I get a little anxious about the flipping. Frittatas are great because all you have to do is cook your favorite fillings in a pan, add your base, and leave it to the oven to take care of the rest. This breakfast frittata is rich in protein, easy to make, and delicious atop a bed of mixed greens.

1 tablespoon (15 ml) sunflower oil, divided

8 ounces (225 g) frozen shredded potato hash browns

⅛ teaspoon salt

¼ teaspoon black pepper, divided

2 cups (260 g) sliced bell peppers, assorted colors

1 cup (110 g) sliced yellow onion

1 cup (135 g) chickpea flour

⅓ cup (30 g) nutritional yeast

2 tablespoons (16 g) cornstarch

2 teaspoons kala namak (Indian black salt)

1 teaspoon onion powder

½ teaspoon baking powder

¼ teaspoon ground turmeric, optional

14 ounces (425 ml) hot vegetable broth

1 can (15 ounces [425 g]) black beans, drained and rinsed

In a 9-inch (23 cm) cast-iron skillet or oven-safe pan, heat 2 teaspoons of the oil over medium heat. Add the hash browns, pressing gently to flatten them into an even layer. Cook until there is some browning on the first side, about 6 minutes, sprinkling the salt and ⅛ teaspoon pepper over the top while they are cooking. Carefully flip the patty onto a plate and set aside. Preheat the oven to 375°F (190°C, or gas mark 5).

Add the remaining 1 teaspoon oil to the skillet along with the bell peppers and onion, and cook, stirring occasionally, until the onions are nearly translucent, about 5 minutes, then remove from the pan and set aside. While the peppers and onions are cooking, whisk together the chickpea flour, nutritional yeast, cornstarch, kala namak, onion powder, baking powder, and turmeric, if using, in a large bowl. Pour the hot vegetable broth into the chickpea flour mixture and whisk until combined.

Slide the hash brown patty, uncooked side down, back into the skillet, then top with the black beans and pepper-onion mixture. Whisk the chickpea mixture to recombine (don't worry about how thin it is) and pour it over the top. Place the skillet in the oven and bake for 33 to 35 minutes, or until the top is matte and slightly firm.

Remove the skillet from the oven and let cool on a rack for 15 to 20 minutes before serving. If storing for later, wait 30 minutes before cutting the frittata into quarters. Transfer to 4 storage containers and store in the refrigerator for up to 7 days or in the freezer for up to 3 months (allow to defrost completely in the refrigerator before reheating).

Note

If you don't have an oven-safe skillet or pan, brown the hash browns on the stovetop as instructed, then transfer them to a pie dish or springform pan before assembling. I love adding ½ cup (56 g) of vegan cheddar shreds to the top of the frittata before baking for an extra layer of flavor.

Instant Pot Rice Pudding

YIELD: 4 SERVINGS

Oats have a special place in my heart, but this brown rice pudding is a welcome change of pace—and it comes together so easily in an Instant Pot! Comforting but not over-the-top heavy, this pudding is made even better with fresh fruits and little cacao nibs.

1¾ cups (415 ml) water

1½ cups (285 g) short-grain brown rice

2 cinnamon sticks

1 teaspoon vanilla extract

1 orange

1 can (13.5 ounces [400 ml]) light coconut milk

¼ cup (60 ml) maple syrup

2 cups (340 g) sliced strawberries

2 cups (290 g) blackberries

4 teaspoons (15 g) cacao nibs

Combine the water, rice, cinnamon sticks, and vanilla in an Instant Pot or pressure cooker. Slice the peel off the orange in large pieces and add the strips to the pot. Secure the lid and bring the pot to high pressure, then cook for 20 minutes. Turn off the heat and let sit for 10 minutes before quick-releasing the remaining pressure. While the rice is cooking, chop the orange into small pieces, taking care to remove any seeds, and set aside.

Discard the orange peels and cinnamon sticks, then stir in the coconut milk and maple syrup. Simmer over low heat for 5 minutes. Divide the pudding between 4 bowls or storage containers, then top with reserved oranges, strawberries, blackberries, and cacao nibs. The pudding can be stored in the refrigerator for up to 7 days or in the freezer for up to 2 months.

Note

To save money, keep frozen berries in your freezer all year long. They're perfect for recipes like this, where it's not imperative to use fresh berries.

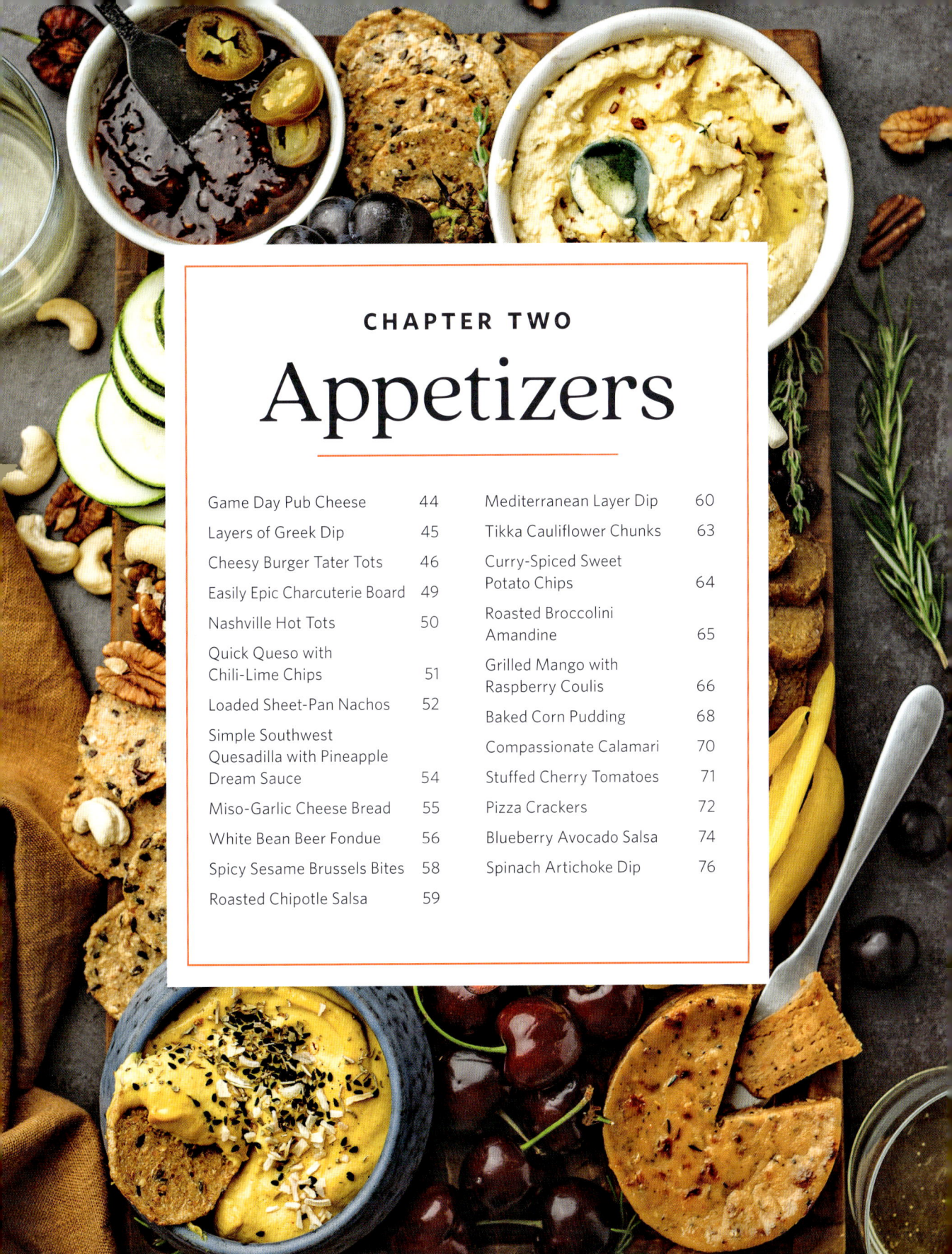

CHAPTER TWO

Appetizers

Game Day Pub Cheese

YIELD: 2 CUPS (480 G)

As a kid, my mom always had this cheese from a company called Schuler's in the refrigerator during the holidays. This is a re-creation of that cheese. The zippy sharpness is addictive. I have taken this to several holiday parties and watched it disappear. One Christmas Eve in Harlem, I watched as the only other vegan at the party pulled up a chair to the hors d'oeuvre table and single-handedly cleared out this dish, cracker after cracker. As usual, I came prepared with backup.

1 cup (137 g) raw cashews, soaked overnight or boiled in water for 10 minutes, drained and rinsed

½ cup (120 ml) vegan lager

¼ cup (60 ml) water

1 tablespoon (15 g) white wine vinegar

2 teaspoons (14 g) maple syrup

¼ cup (35 g) sauerkraut

¼ cup (60 g) tahini

1 tablespoon (16 g) white miso

2 tablespoons (30 g) Dijon mustard

1 teaspoon smoked paprika

1 teaspoon garlic powder

¾ teaspoon ground turmeric

½ teaspoon onion powder

½ teaspoon sea salt

Combine the cashews, lager, water, vinegar, maple syrup, sauerkraut, tahini, miso, Dijon mustard, smoked paprika, garlic powder, turmeric, onion powder, and salt in a blender.

Start the blender speed on low, slowly incorporating the ingredients into the fold. Once the ingredients begin to move, gradually increase the speed. Stop the blender and scrape the sides down as needed to get everything into the mix. Blend until creamy and smooth.

Serve with crackers or vegetables.

Note

Cashew sauces tend to thicken when they sit in the refrigerator. I'm always impatient, and it's hard for me to wait for this cheese. If you are going to take this to a party, make it 2 days in advance so it thickens slightly and is servable as a spread.

Layers of Greek Dip

YIELD: 8 SERVINGS

The fresh tangy flavors of Greek cuisine always entice me. What's better than scooping up a bunch of layered flavors with some veggies or chips for a fun appetizer? This is great for parties as it's not the traditional seven-layer dip people are expecting. It's loaded with different textures—from the creamy hummus to the crunchy cucumber—for a very satisfying bite!

½ teaspoon dried dill

1 container (5 ounces [140 g]) plain vegan yogurt

1 container (10 ounces [280 g]) store-bought hummus

½ cup (64 g) kalamata olives, pitted and roughly chopped

½ cup (100 g) diced cucumber, skin on

½ cup (75 g) grape tomatoes, roughly chopped

½ cup (57 g) vegan block feta or mozzarella, cut into ½-inch (1 cm) cubes

Olive oil (optional)

Sea salt and black pepper (optional)

3 scallions, thinly sliced

Tortilla chips, pita chips, warm pita bread, or sliced vegetables

Add the dill to the yogurt and mix until well combined. You can even add it in the yogurt container if it's a single serve. Spread the hummus on a small platter (5 × 8-inch [13 × 20 cm]), shallow serving dish, or standard-size dinner plate. Top the hummus with the yogurt mixture followed by the olives, cucumbers, tomatoes, and feta. Drizzle with olive oil and sprinkle with salt and pepper (if using). Sprinkle with scallions and serve with chips, bread, or vegetables.

Cheesy Burger Tater Tots

YIELD: 8 SERVINGS

Tater tots are a classic favorite for everyone, with their crisp and crunchy outsides and pillows of warm potato in the middle. I squeal with delight every time a restaurant offers tots as a potato option. Okay, maybe not squeal, but I do get excited. So why not top some tots with nostalgic flavors everyone loves—like the flavors of a cheeseburger! Just pop it on a sheet pan and you have dinner or an appetizer to wow friends and family in thirty minutes.

4 cups (half of a 32-ounce [905g] bag) frozen tater tots

½ teaspoon Old Bay Seasoning (optional)

1 cup (110 g) frozen vegan ground beef or crumbled vegan sausage

½ cup (80 g) roughly chopped white onion

½ cup (90 g) diced tomato

¼ cup (60 g) sweet pickle relish

¾ cup (88 g) vegan cheddar shreds

Mustard

Ketchup

Quick Thousand Island dressing (optional, see Note)

2 scallions, chopped (optional)

Preheat the oven to 425°F (220°C, or gas mark 7). Line a sheet pan with parchment paper.

Spread the tater tots out on the prepared sheet pan and sprinkle with Old Bay Seasoning (if using). Bake for 20 minutes, remove from the oven, and flip the tater tots with a spatula. Position the tater tots close together so they are touching to minimize the toppings falling through to the sheet pan. Top the tater tots with ground beef, onion, tomatoes, relish, and cheese. Bake for 10 to 12 minutes, until the cheese is melted and the tater tots have turned golden brown.

Drizzle tater tots with mustard, ketchup, or dressing, and sprinkle with chopped scallions (if using).

Note

Create your epic and turn this into Big Mac Tots with a quick Thousand Island dressing. In a bowl combine ½ cup (115 g) vegan mayonnaise, 2 tablespoons (30 g) sweet pickle relish, 1 tablespoon (15 g) yellow mustard, and 1 tablespoon (15 g) ketchup. Drizzle the dressing over this recipe instead of mustard or ketchup or use it on burgers as desired. Keep refrigerated for up to 2 weeks in an airtight container.

Easily Epic Charcuterie Board

YIELD: 1 CHARCUTERIE BOARD

This is it. The moment to impress your nonvegan friends by creating an epic charcuterie board your guests will swoon over! It's all in the presentation. Don't forget to add a mix of bright fruits and vegetables to complete the look of your board. As always, I encourage you to omit items you don't love and add your favorite items. If vegan meats aren't your thing, just double up the veggies—a charcuterie board is absolutely still in your future! There are suggested measurements below, but ultimately you have to build this according to the size of the board you have. Now go . . . put the CUTE in CharCUTErie!

APPETIZERS

2 dips: ½ cup (120 g) store-bought hummus and ½ cup (165 g) jelly or jam

1 cup (128 g) mixed olives

2 vegan cheeses: pub cheese and other cheese (block, spread, or wheel)

2 vegan meats: vegan deli slices, vegan pepperoni, prepared and thinly sliced vegan sausage links

3 cups fruit (pick 3, 1 cup of each): blackberries, apple slices, pear slices, grapes, raspberries, cherries, strawberries, or blueberries

2 vegetables: carrots, cucumber, bell peppers, or zucchini, cut into sticks or thinly sliced

1 box raw or vegan crackers

½ cup (55 g) pecan halves

½ cup (68 g) raw or lightly salted cashews

½ cup (57 g) dried cherries or dried fruit of choice

Fresh herbs, such as rosemary or thyme

Add the hummus, jam, and olives to small bowls that fit on the board. Place the bowls in a triangle formation on the board with 1 in the center and the other 2 at the corners. Add the cheese to the other 2 corners of the board.

Now comes the fun. Fill in the board with vegan meats, fruits, vegetables, crackers, nuts, and dried fruit. Add serving spoons or cheese knives as needed, and garnish with sprigs of fresh herbs for the finishing touch.

Make this an hour before serving. If you choose apple or pear slices, toss them quickly in lemon or lime juice to avoid oxidizing. Cover with plastic wrap and store in the refrigerator until the first guest arrives.

Note

If you don't have a fancy cheese board, simply cover a sheet pan with a fitted piece of parchment paper for a fun, rustic look! Don't break the bank buying fancy cheese knives. If all you have is a butter knife, work with what you've got! I like to use "fancier" jams and jellies for these boards, such as a spiced pear or apricot. If you can't find one, just pour a little juice from a pickled jalapeño jar into some raspberry preserves and BAM, jalapeño raspberry!

Nashville Hot Tots

YIELD: 6 SERVINGS

"Nashville Hot" has been a craze lately! And I love some spice and tater tots, so I thought no better time to pair these perfect little crunchy pillow puffs of potato with the irresistible Nashville hot spice mixture. While I try to mix ingredients with spices on a sheet pan when I can to eliminate dishes, it is best to mix this recipe in a couple of bowls so the variety of spices get well incorporated into all the tater tots.

4 cups (half of a 32-ounce [907 g] bag) frozen tater tots

Cooking spray

1 teaspoon cayenne pepper

2 tablespoons (20 g) light brown sugar

2 teaspoons (5 g) paprika

1 teaspoon garlic powder

1 teaspoon sea salt

½ teaspoon black pepper

Vegan salad dressing for dipping (optional)

Preheat the oven to 450°F (230°C, or gas mark 8). Line a large sheet pan with parchment paper.

Add the tater tots to a bowl and spray with cooking spray. Toss to coat and then spray again, covering all tots with a mist of oil. In a small bowl, whisk together the cayenne, brown sugar, paprika, garlic powder, salt, and pepper. Add half of the spice mixture to the bowl of tots and toss to combine. Add the second half of the mixture, and continue to toss tots until all pieces are coated.

Transfer the tots to the prepared sheet pan and bake for 15 minutes. Flip the tots and bake for 10 to 12 minutes, until they are crispy and have darkened in color.

Serve with your favorite vegan dipping sauce.

Quick Queso with Chili-Lime Chips

YIELD: 6 TO 8 SERVINGS

Chain restaurants and queso: Get it together and offer a vegan version already! It's so easy! Never fret, you can now make some for you and your friends lickity-split using one pot on the stovetop. Then pick your adventure. Just open the bag of chips and serve alongside the quick queso or add some tangy spice to your store-bought chips with a lil' action in the oven. Adjust the amount of chili powder on the chips to your desired amount of heat.

FOR THE QUESO

¼ cup (32 g) all-purpose or gluten-free all-purpose flour

¼ cup (59 ml) canola oil

¼ cup (20 g) nutritional yeast

2 tablespoons (24 g) taco seasoning, plus more to taste

1 teaspoon sea salt

3 tablespoons (45 g) tahini

1 tablespoon (15 ml) white wine vinegar

1 tablespoon (15 g) Dijon mustard

2 cups (475 ml) nondairy milk

1 can (10 ounces [280 g]) diced tomatoes with green chilies, drained (I prefer Rotel brand.)

FOR THE CHILI-LIME CHIPS

1 bag (12 ounces [340 g]) tortilla chips

1 teaspoon chili powder, plus more to taste

1 lime, halved

To make the queso

Add the flour and canola oil to a saucepan over medium heat. Whisk continuously until the mixture is creamy and smooth and thickens just slightly. Lower the heat and add the nutritional yeast, taco seasoning, salt, tahini, vinegar, and Dijon. Whisk until well combined. Add the milk and whisk to combine everything until you have a faint orange-colored queso. Add the tomatoes and mix until well combined. Bring the queso to a bubble, then lower the heat to a simmer for a few minutes just to blend the flavors, stirring frequently to avoid sticking to the pan.

To make the chili-lime chips

Preheat the oven to 350°F (180°C, or gas mark 4). Line a large sheet pan with parchment paper. Arrange the bag of tortilla chips in a single layer and sprinkle with chili powder, to taste. Squeeze the lime halves over the chips, getting lime juice on as many pieces as you can. Bake for 6 to 8 minutes, or until the chips have browned slightly and the lime juice dries.

Serve the warm queso with chips. To reheat the queso, set it over low heat until warmed throughout. This will keep in the refrigerator for up to 1 week.

Note

For a heartier queso, omit half of the tomatoes and add ½ cup (50 g) vegan sausage or chorizo roughly chopped or crumbled.

Loaded Sheet-Pan Nachos

YIELD: 6 TO 8 SERVINGS

Nachos are EVERYTHING! Am I right?! The creative part of making nachos is my favorite part. Tortilla chips are like a blank canvas to carry bite-size parcels of food to your food trap (aka mouth). Make this recipe first as is, and then come back to it and omit ingredients you don't like or add your favorites! As long as it's slathered with some cheese at the end, you can't go wrong.

PLANT-BASED SIMPLE

1 bag (12 ounces [340 g]) tortilla chips

1 cup (70 g) shredded red cabbage

1 can (15 ounces [425 g]) black beans, drained and rinsed

½ cup (82 g) frozen or fresh corn

½ red bell pepper, roughly chopped

1 can (2.25 ounces [64 g]) sliced black olives, drained

1 cup (115 g) vegan cheese shreds

1 cup (260 g) store-bought salsa

1 avocado, peeled and chopped (optional)

Vegan sour cream

Sliced jalapeños, canned, jarred, or fresh (optional)

3 scallions, roughly chopped

Preheat the oven to 400°F (200°C, or gas mark 6). Line a 11 × 16-inch (28 × 41 cm) rimmed sheet pan with parchment paper.

Spread a single layer of tortilla chips over the entire sheet pan. Evenly disperse the cabbage, black beans, corn, bell pepper, and black olives until the tortilla chips are completely covered. Sprinkle or drizzle cheese over the top.

Bake the nachos for 10 to 12 minutes, or until the cheese is melted and the edges of the chips on the outside of the sheet pan have just browned. Be careful not to burn the tortilla chips. Some store-bought vegan cheeses can be finicky. If needed, turn the oven up to broil for just 1 to 2 minutes to give the cheese that little extra push to melt.

Remove the nachos from the oven and top with salsa, avocado, sour cream, and jalapeños (if using). Sprinkle with scallions and serve directly from the sheet pan. Warn your guests that the sheet pan is hot.

Note

Not making this for a party? Split the recipe in half for a smaller crowd or dinner for two, easy peasy.

Simple Southwest Quesadilla with Pineapple Dream Sauce

YIELD: 6 QUESADILLAS

Back in my days as a server at a place called Bennigan's, they had these Southwest eggrolls with creamy pineapple dipping sauce that my sister was bananas for. So, this is for my sister, a much easier version to make combining vegan cheese, crispy vegetables, and optional tofu, seitan, or vegan chicken on corn tortillas baked in the oven all at once. No frying required. Serve it up with plain salsa or go the extra mile and make this decadent, easy pineapple dipping sauce to wow your in-laws or whomever.

FOR THE SOUTHWEST QUESADILLA

1 red bell pepper, roughly chopped

½ red onion, roughly chopped

1 cup (164 g) fresh or frozen corn

1¼ cups (135 g) vegan cheddar shreds

2 teaspoons (4 g) ground cumin

2 teaspoons (4 g) chili powder

1 teaspoon sea salt, plus more for sprinkling

12 (6-inch [15 cm]) corn tortillas

Cooking spray

Chopped fresh cilantro (optional)

FOR THE CREAMY PINEAPPLE DREAM SAUCE

½ cup (115 g) vegan mayonnaise

2 tablespoons (33 g) store-bought salsa of choice

3 tablespoons (32 g) canned crushed pineapple, drained with liquid reserved

Preheat the oven to 400°F (200°C, or gas mark 6). Line a large sheet pan with parchment paper.

To make the Southwest quesadilla
Add the bell pepper, onion, corn, cheese, cumin, chili powder, and salt to a bowl. Toss to combine. Lay 6 corn tortillas on the sheet pan. Add ½ cup (120 ml) scoop of the mixture to each tortilla and top with the remaining 6 corn tortillas.

Spray the tortillas lightly with cooking spray and sprinkle with a touch more salt, if desired. Bake for 10 minutes and then flip each quesadilla. Spray again lightly with cooking spray and sprinkle sparingly with salt if desired. Bake for 10 minutes, until golden brown and cheese has melted.

To make the creamy pineapple dream sauce
Mix the mayonnaise, salsa, and pineapple in a bowl until well combined.

Remove the quesadillas from the oven and sprinkle with cilantro (if using). Cut each one into quarters (4 triangles). Transfer to a serving plate, and serve with pineapple dream sauce or salsa of choice.

Note

This is a fast and efficient hot app to serve at parties. When they come out of the oven, cut each quesadilla into 4 pieces. Place the sauce in a bowl in the middle of a round serving platter and then fan the quesadilla pieces out around the sauce. Sprinkle the quesadilla pieces with freshly chopped cilantro for a little extra flair.

Miso-Garlic Cheese Bread

YIELD: 24 PIECES

This is an amped-up version of the frozen garlic bread from the supermarket. For me it screams perfection from the first bite of its flaky crispy crust down to its melty buttery chew. Make it as is and then create your own variations to suit your taste!

¼ cup (55 g) vegan butter, soft at room temperature

1 tablespoon (16 g) miso

1 tablespoon (5 g) nutritional yeast

1 teaspoon garlic powder

1 (12-inch [30 cm]) baguette, halved and scored into 12 pieces, 24 pieces total (see Note)

½ cup (57 g) vegan mozzarella shreds, plus more to taste

½ teaspoon Italian seasoning

Crushed red pepper (optional)

Preheat the broiler in the oven. DO NOT line a sheet pan with parchment paper.

In a small bowl, cream together the butter, miso, nutritional yeast, and garlic powder until well combined.

Lay each side of the baguette on a sheet pan with the scored insides facing up. Spread the mixture on the baguettes, dividing the mixture evenly between the 2 pieces. Sprinkle each one with ¼ cup (26 g) mozzarella shreds. Add more shreds if desired. Finish by sprinkling each baguette with ¼ teaspoon Italian seasoning and the desired amount of crushed red pepper (if using).

Place in the broiler for 3 minutes. Rotate the pan and broil for another 3 minutes, until the butter mixture underneath the cheese browns and the cheese has melted. Remove from the oven and briefly let cool to the touch before breaking pieces off and transferring them to a serving platter or plate.

Remember, all broilers have different intensity. Keep an eye on the bread. If you find after the first 3 minutes the butter has browned and the cheese is melted, there is no need to continue broiling.

Note

Traditionally bread is scored before it's baked to allow it to expand during baking. Here, we are scoring it to precut the bread into pieces so you can easily pull pieces apart after baking. Start this recipe by cutting the 12-inch (30 cm) baguette in half lengthwise and placing the outside of the baguettes on a flat surface. Use a sharp knife to slice into the bread, but don't slice all the way through when you reach the bottom, leaving just the outer crust connected. Pieces should be 1 inch (2.5 cm) long creating 12 pieces in each side of the baguette for a total of 24 pieces.

White Bean Beer Fondue

YIELD: 4 SERVINGS

Fondue makes for a fun appetizer to be shared among friends, whether for a dinner party or a game night. This creamy, low-fat fondue is a delicious crowd-pleaser, especially with its beer-tinged aroma.

FOR THE FONDUE

¼ cup (35 g) raw cashews, soaked in warm water for 30 minutes

1 can (15 ounces [425 g]) white beans, undrained

½ cup (120 ml) unsweetened soy-free nondairy milk

½ cup (120 ml) ale or lager (gluten-free, if necessary)

¼ cup (15 g) nutritional yeast

2 tablespoons (15 g) tapioca starch

2 cloves garlic, peeled

2 teaspoons coconut vinegar

1 teaspoon apple cider vinegar

1 teaspoon Dijon mustard

1 teaspoon salt

FOR THE DIPPING

1½ cups (107 g) broccoli florets

1½ cups (195 g) carrot sticks

1½ cups (75 g) toasted cubed bread (gluten-free, if necessary)

1 cup (150 g) cubed green apple

1 cup (60 g) pretzels (gluten-free, if necessary)

Drain and rinse the cashews and then place them in a blender along with the white beans (plus the liquid from the beans), soy-free nondairy milk, beer, nutritional yeast, tapioca starch, garlic, both vinegars, and mustard. Puree the mixture until very smooth and transfer the cheese sauce to a large saucepan.

Bring the mixture to a simmer over medium heat, whisking frequently to make sure the bottom doesn't burn. The fondue will thicken, and you want it to get hot so that the tapioca starch completely dissolves. Whisk until the fondue leaves a thick coating of sauce on the whisk or a spoon when dipped into it. Add the salt and stir.

Transfer the fondue to a small slow cooker, fondue pot, or glass bowl for serving. Place the broccoli florets, carrot sticks, toast cubes, apple cubes, and pretzels on a serving tray with skewers for dipping.

Spicy Sesame Brussels Bites

YIELD: 4 SMALL SERVINGS

Brussels sprouts are the vegetable that your mom used to completely overcook for holidays—which made everyone hate them—but that are now making a comeback in a huge way. There's just something about these "mini-cabbages," as I call them, which makes them my favorite choice for roasting and serving to the masses.

1½ pounds (680 g) Brussels sprouts, trimmed but kept whole

2 tablespoons (28 ml) toasted sesame oil

1 teaspoon crushed red pepper flakes

¼ teaspoon salt

⅛ teaspoon ground ginger

1 tablespoon (15 ml) rice vinegar

1 tablespoon (15 ml) agave nectar

2 teaspoons sesame seeds, toasted

1 teaspoon liquid aminos or tamari

Preheat the oven to 375°F (190°C, or gas mark 5) and line a baking sheet with parchment paper. In a large bowl, toss together the Brussels sprouts, sesame oil, red pepper flakes, salt, and ginger. Spread the sprouts out on the lined baking sheet.

Bake for 25 minutes, stirring halfway through so that the sprouts roast evenly. Once roasted, place them back in the large bowl and toss them with the rice vinegar, agave nectar, toasted sesame seeds, and liquid aminos. Serve hot.

Roasted Chipotle Salsa

YIELD: 8 SERVINGS

There is no reason to resort to mediocre store-bought salsas when you can make a better version at home. Fuel your chip addiction with this restaurant-style salsa, made up of roasted tomatoes, smoky chipotle chile powder, and fresh lime juice.

2 pounds (910 g) tomatoes

2 ounces (55 g) fresh jalapeños

½ cup (80 g) chopped red onion

¼ cup (4 g) fresh cilantro

1 teaspoon lime juice

½ teaspoon ground chipotle chile powder

½ teaspoon salt, or to taste

Prepare a hot fire in a grill (350°F, or 180°C) and oil the grill grates. Grill the tomatoes and jalapeños until charred on all sides. Remove them from the grill, place on a plate, and cover with a larger plate or a bowl.

After about 15 minutes, peel the skins off the tomatoes and jalapeños and remove the stems (for less spicy heat, remove the seeds also). Place them in a food processor with the red onion, cilantro, lime juice, chipotle chile powder, and salt and then pulse until slightly chunky.

Transfer the salsa to a large jar and refrigerate for at least 1 hour before serving. The salsa will keep for up to 2 weeks in the refrigerator.

Mediterranean Layer Dip

YIELD: 8 SERVINGS

Why choose between different types of dip to bring to a party when you can combine the creaminess of hummus with the salty, chewy texture of tapenade and finish it off with a fresh basil pesto? Serve this pretty, layered dip with pita chips or fresh vegetable spears and sticks.

FOR THE RED LENTIL HUMMUS

⅔ cup (128 g) dried red lentils

1½ cups (355 ml) water

2 tablespoons (30 g) tahini

1 tablespoon (15 ml) olive oil

1 tablespoon (15 ml) lemon juice

1 teaspoon ground cumin

1 clove garlic, peeled

¼ to ½ teaspoon sea salt

FOR THE PESTO

3 cups (60 g) arugula

1½ cups (60 g) fresh basil leaves, plus a few more for garnish

¼ cup (35 g) pine nuts

1 or 2 cloves garlic, peeled

3 tablespoons (45 ml) olive oil

2 tablespoons (28 ml) lemon juice

¼ teaspoon sea salt

Black pepper, to taste

FOR THE OLIVE TAPENADE

½ cup (85 g) pitted black olives

½ cup (85 g) pitted green olives

1 tablespoon (8 g) capers

1 tablespoon (15 ml) lemon juice

1 clove garlic, peeled

1 teaspoon nutritional yeast

⅛ teaspoon black pepper

To make the red lentil hummus

Place the red lentils and water in a small pot and bring to a boil over high heat. Reduce the heat to medium-low and simmer the lentils until cooked, about 20 minutes. Drain any excess water.

In a food processor with an S-blade, pulse the cooked lentils with the tahini, olive oil, lemon juice, cumin, garlic, and sea salt until very smooth. Set the hummus aside and rinse out the processor.

To make the pesto

Place all the ingredients in the food processor and pulse until mostly smooth; you may need to scrape the sides with a spatula and pulse more for an even consistency. Set the pesto aside and rinse out the processor.

To make the olive tapenade

Place all the ingredients in the food processor and pulse until all pieces are the size of small grains; you don't want this to be as smooth as a paste.

Layer the dips in a glass bowl, starting with the hummus, then adding the pesto, and last adding the tapenade. Garnish with fresh basil leaves and serve.

Tikka Cauliflower Chunks

YIELD: 4 SERVINGS

Serving cauliflower at a party may sound like an idea that's been played out, but when you put a tangy tikka spin on it, this version will bring back the shine to any veggie tray!

1 cup (230 g) plain coconut milk yogurt

2 tablespoons (28 ml) lemon juice

1 tablespoon (6 g) minced fresh ginger

2 cloves garlic, minced

1 tablespoon (6 g) minced fresh jalapeño

1 teaspoon ground turmeric

½ teaspoon ground cumin

½ teaspoon garam masala

½ teaspoon sea salt

Pinch of black pepper

2 pounds (910 g) cauliflower, cut into florets

¼ cup (54 g) coconut oil, melted

3 tablespoons (3 g) chopped fresh cilantro

Preheat the oven to 400°F (200°C, or gas mark 6) and line a baking sheet with parchment paper.

In a food processor or blender, puree the yogurt, lemon juice, ginger, garlic, jalapeño, turmeric, cumin, garam masala, sea salt, and pepper together until mostly smooth. In a large bowl, toss the sauce with the cauliflower florets until they are evenly coated and then spread them out over the parchment paper.

Roast the cauliflower for 20 to 25 minutes, flipping the florets halfway through as to not burn one side. Once the cauliflower is roasted and lightly browned, take the baking sheet out of the oven and brush the florets with the melted coconut oil.

Place the cauliflower in a serving bowl, sprinkle the cilantro on top, and serve along with toothpicks or a serving spoon.

APPETIZERS

Curry-Spiced Sweet Potato Chips

YIELD: 4 SMALL SERVINGS

Sweet potato chips are delicious in their own right, but by spicing them up with a curry blend and a kick from cayenne pepper and pairing them with a sriracha aioli, these chips turn delightfully addictive.

FOR THE CHIPS

1 pound (455 g) sweet potatoes, peeled

2 tablespoons (28 ml) olive oil

1 tablespoon (6 g) yellow curry powder

½ teaspoon salt

⅛ teaspoon ground cinnamon

⅛ teaspoon smoked paprika

⅛ teaspoon cayenne pepper

FOR THE SPICY AIOLI

¼ cup (60 g) vegan mayonnaise

1 tablespoon (15 ml) sriracha hot sauce

¼ teaspoon garlic powder

To make the chips

Preheat the oven to 350°F (180°C, or gas mark 4) and line 2 baking sheets with parchment paper.

Using a mandolin or sharp knife, cut the sweet potatoes into slices about ⅛ inch (3 mm) thick. Place all the slices in a large bowl, drizzle with the olive oil, and toss until they are evenly coated.

Spread the slices out over the baking sheets, making sure that they are not overlapping. In a small bowl, whisk together the curry powder, salt, cinnamon, smoked paprika, and cayenne. Sprinkle half of the mixture over the 2 baking sheets of sweet potatoes and bake them for 10 minutes.

Take the chips out of the oven, carefully flip them over, sprinkle with the remaining spice mixture, and bake for 10 more minutes or until lightly browned. Place the baking sheets on cooling racks for 10 minutes. When the chips have hardened a bit, transfer them to a serving bowl.

To make the spicy aioli

Stir together the vegan mayonnaise, sriracha, and garlic powder until combined. Serve with the chips.

Roasted Broccolini Amandine

YIELD: 4 SMALL SERVINGS

You really can't go wrong with roasting broccolini. It's sweeter than broccoli and it tastes excellent when paired with garlic and toasted almonds.

¾ pound (340 g) broccolini

2 tablespoons (28 ml) olive oil

3 cloves garlic, thinly sliced

¼ teaspoon dried oregano

⅓ cup (32 g) sliced almonds

¼ teaspoon salt

Pinch of black pepper

Preheat the oven to 375°F (190°C, or gas mark 5) and line a baking sheet with parchment paper.

In a large bowl, toss together the broccolini, olive oil, garlic, and oregano and then spread the mixture out on the baking sheet in a single layer.

Bake for 10 minutes and then take the baking sheet out of the oven and sprinkle the almond slices, salt, and pepper over the top. Return to the oven and bake for 5 more minutes to brown the almonds slightly. Serve hot.

Grilled Mango with Raspberry Coulis

YIELD: 4 SERVINGS

Need a healthy snack that is packed with great flavors from grilled mango, sweet raspberries, and tart orange juice? I've got the perfect dish for you.

6 ounces (170 g) fresh raspberries

¼ cup (60 ml) orange juice

2 tablespoons (28 ml) water

2 tablespoons (28 ml) organic cane sugar

½ teaspoon grated orange zest

Pinch of salt

3 pounds (1.4 kg) mango, seeded, peeled, and sliced into ¼-inch (6 mm)-wide strips

Prepare a hot fire in a grill (375°F, or 190°C) and oil the grill grates.

While the grill is heating, place the raspberries, orange juice, water, sugar, orange zest, and salt in a blender and puree until smooth. Strain the mixture through a fine-mesh sieve to remove the raspberry seeds. Simmer the coulis in a small saucepan over medium-low heat for 5 to 7 minutes, stirring occasionally.

Grill the mango slices for 2 to 3 minutes on each side until there are dark grill marks.

Toss the mango in a large bowl with the raspberry coulis and serve.

Note

Experiment with this recipe by trying it out with some of your favorite fruits. Pineapple, peaches, and plantains are all great for grilling.

Baked Corn Pudding

YIELD: 8 SERVINGS

The easiest way to serve this classic dish, which is unlike sweet pudding and closer to a very wet corn bread, is by scooping it with a spoon, hence the name "corn pudding." I couldn't resist including this recipe because it has always been one of my favorite side dishes since I was a youngster.

⅓ cup (80 ml) olive oil

½ cup (60 g) masa harina flour

¼ teaspoon sea salt

1 teaspoon baking powder

⅓ cup (47 g) finely ground cornmeal

¼ cup (60 ml) water

¼ cup (50 g) sugar

5 tablespoons (75 ml) canned coconut milk

2 cups (300 g) fresh or thawed frozen corn kernels

Preheat the oven to 325°F (170°C, or gas mark 3). Lightly grease an 8 × 8-inch (20 × 20 cm) glass baking dish.

Mix all the ingredients together in a large bowl until well combined. Spread into the prepared pan and bake for 50 to 55 minutes or until the edges are lightly golden brown.

Serve by scooping out with a spoon or small ice cream scoop. Best if eaten hot or slightly above room temperature.

Note

Spice things up by adding finely minced jalapeños and some cumin, chili powder, and black pepper.

Compassionate Calamari

YIELD: 8 SERVINGS

This dish is deliciously crispy and reminiscent of actual calamari. But happily, no squid were harmed in the making of this terrific appetizer.

Vegetable oil, for cooking

FOR THE COATING

3 tablespoons (21 g) flax-seed meal mixed with 6 tablespoons (90 ml) warm water

¼ cup (60 ml) nondairy milk

¼ teaspoon sea salt

FOR THE DRY BATTER

½ cup (30 g) brown rice flour

⅓ cup (47 g) ground yellow cornmeal

1 teaspoon dulse granules or flakes

FOR THE WET BATTER

1 cup (140 g) finely ground yellow cornmeal

1½ cups (350 ml) nondairy milk

6 large king oyster mushrooms, tough bottoms removed, sliced into ¼- to ½-inch (6 mm to 1.3 cm)-wide strips

Sea salt, to taste

FOR THE GARLIC TARTER SAUCE

½ cup (120 ml) vegan mayonnaise

2 teaspoons sweet relish

1 teaspoon finely minced garlic

1 tablespoon (15 ml) lemon juice

Pour the oil to a depth of 5 inches (13 cm) into a deep fryer or deep pot and heat to 360°F (182°C).

To make the coating
Mix all the coating ingredients together in a small bowl.

To make the dry batter
Sift together all the dry batter ingredients in a small bowl.

To make the wet batter
In a medium-size bowl, whisk the cornmeal and nondairy milk together until a thick batter forms.

I find it easiest to have each mixture in a small dish in the order given so it's easy to dip the mushroom slices assembly style. Make sure your oil is at temperature before attempting to dip your mushrooms because it will be difficult to set them down once they are coated.

Dip 1 mushroom slice first into the coating, then into the dry batter, and finally into the wet batter, letting any excess drip off. The mushroom should be evenly coated. Drop immediately into the hot oil and quickly repeat with a few more mushrooms until you run out of room in your fryer. Fry for 6 minutes or until dark golden brown. Remove with a skimmer and transfer to a folded brown paper bag or paper towels to absorb any excess grease. Season lightly with salt, if desired. Repeat until each mushroom slice has been cooked. Serve immediately with the dipping sauce and enjoy!

To make the garlic tarter sauce
Stir together all the ingredients in a small bowl until thoroughly combined.

Stuffed Cherry Tomatoes

YIELD: 13 APPETIZER-SIZE SERVINGS, 2 TOMATOES EACH

This is an irresistible finger food that's to be eaten hot from the oven. Well, not too hot because you'll burn your mouth; let 'em cool for a few minutes before offering them up for munching.

1 cup (120 g) chopped walnuts

1 tablespoon (2.5 g) fresh sage

2 cloves garlic, minced

½ cup (75 g) chopped onion

1 tablespoon (15 g) apricot jam

1 teaspoon sea salt

26 cherry tomatoes

Olive oil, for drizzling

Preheat the oven to 350°F (180°C, or gas mark 4).

In a food processor, combine the walnuts, sage, garlic, onion, jam, and salt. Pulse several times until a paste is formed.

Slice the tops off the cherry tomatoes. Using a small spoon, scoop out the seeds of each cherry tomato and discard the seedy filling. Fill each tomato with the walnut paste and replace the tomato cap. I like to overstuff mine so that the cap just barely sits on top of the filling. Arrange snugly in a small baking dish so the caps remain upright. Drizzle lightly with olive oil.

Bake for about 30 minutes. Let cool briefly and then serve immediately.

Note

Prepare these appetizers ahead of time. For seamless serving, don't bake them until the guests arrive.

Pizza Crackers

YIELD: ABOUT 70 CRACKERS, 3 CRACKERS PER SERVING

I created these crackers to satisfy my late-night munchies, and every time I finish off a big batch, their addictive pizza flavor just leaves me craving more!

2 cups (260 g) chickpea flour

½ cup (65 g) sorghum flour, plus more for rolling

½ cup (65 g) potato starch

½ cup (65 g) nutritional yeast

1 teaspoon xanthan gum

1 teaspoon sea salt

2 to 3 teaspoons ground pizza seasoning, plus more for sprinkling

⅓ cup (80 ml) olive oil

¼ cup (60 g) tomato paste

¾ cup (180 ml) cold water

Preheat the oven to 350°F (180°C, or gas mark 4).

In a large bowl, combine the chickpea flour, sorghum flour, potato starch, nutritional yeast, xanthan gum, salt, and pizza seasoning until well mixed.

Using a large spoon, stir in the olive oil, tomato paste, and cold water. Mix until very well combined. Turn the dough out onto a lightly floured surface and knead just until the dough is uniform in texture and color.

Add a little more flour to your rolling surface and pat out the dough to about 1 inch (2.5 cm) thick. Sprinkle the top with a touch more sorghum flour and flip over.

With a lightly floured rolling pin, roll out the dough until it is about ⅛ inch (3 mm) thick. Use a circular cookie cutter or a pizza wheel to cut out 1½-inch (3.8 cm) shapes of dough. Sprinkle with additional pizza seasoning.

Use a flat metal spatula to scoop up the shapes and place on an ungreased baking sheet, spacing them about 1 inch (2.5 cm) apart.

Bake for about 30 minutes, flipping once halfway through the cooking time. The crackers will have a reddish hue (from the tomato paste) but should be slightly puffy and golden brown on both sides when they are done. Depending on the size of your baking sheets and oven, you may need to make 2 or 3 batches of crackers.

Let cool completely. Stored in an airtight container, these will keep for up to a week.

Note

I love pairing these crackers with my Quick Garlic Herb Dip (pictured). To make, simply blend together 1 cup (230 g) nondairy cream cheese and ½ cup (115 g) nondairy sour cream in a bowl. Stir in 2 teaspoons garlic powder, 2 tablespoons (15 g) chopped chives, 1 teaspoon each minced fresh basil and oregano, and ½ teaspoon lemon zest. Garnish with pizza seasoning and extra chopped chives.

Blueberry Avocado Salsa

YIELD: 3 SERVINGS

This fruity salsa is sure to delight as well as intrigue. It's best if made with fresh blueberries when in season, but frozen will work just fine.

2 large tomatoes, quartered

2 cups (290 g) fresh blueberries

2 tablespoons (30 ml) lime juice, plus extra for drizzling

¼ cup (40 g) chopped scallions

½ cup (8 g) chopped fresh cilantro

1 teaspoon sea salt, or more to taste

1 jalapeño pepper, stemmed, seeded, and chopped (leave the seeds in if you like more heat)

1 ripe avocado, peeled, pitted, and cut into small chunks

Combine the tomatoes, blueberries, 2 tablespoons (30 ml) lime juice, scallion, cilantro, salt, and jalapeño in a food processor and pulse a few times. Transfer to a bowl. Drizzle the remaining lime juice over the avocado chunks. Add to the salsa and stir to combine. Add a touch more salt if desired. Serve immediately.

Note

This salsa should keep up to 1 week if stored properly in an airtight container.

Spinach Artichoke Dip

YIELD: 8 SERVINGS

As a frequenter of chain restaurants in my youth, I cannot imagine what my life would be like without the occasional decadent dish of spinach artichoke dip. This richly flavored dip is great for movie night when served along with your favorite tortilla chips.

2½ cups (425 g) unsweetened cashew cream

½ cup (110 g) vegan mayonnaise

½ cup (65 g) nutritional yeast

3 cloves garlic, minced

2 cups (60 g) packed chopped spinach leaves

1 can (14 ounces [392 g]) large artichoke hearts, chopped

3 scallions, sliced into small rings

1 teaspoon lemon zest

½ teaspoon black pepper

Salt, to taste

Preheat the oven to 350°F (180°C, or gas mark 4).

Stir together the cashew cream, vegan mayonnaise, nutritional yeast, garlic, chopped spinach, chopped artichoke hearts, scallions, lemon zest, and pepper until very well combined. Season with salt. Place in an oven-safe dish.

Bake for 25 minutes. Turn the oven to broil and cook for 2 to 3 minutes, or until the top becomes golden brown and crispy.

Serve hot with your favorite dipping chips or crackers.

Note

If you are hosting a big get-together and plan on serving this dip, you better make a double batch—this stuff goes fast!

Soups & Sandwiches

Very Fast Veggie Lentil Soup

YIELD: 6 TO 8 SERVINGS

Lentils are packed with protein, and vegetables are packed with nutrients. Put them together in a soup and pair it with a delicious grain bowl or salad for lunch and you are set! The creamy texture of the lentils with the soft crunch of freshly cooked vegetables is a surefire delight, especially when mixed with some robust diced tomatoes.

1 tablespoon (15 ml) olive oil

1 onion, diced

2 celery stalks, thinly sliced

2 carrots, peeled and thinly sliced

4 cloves garlic, minced

6 cups (1.4 L) vegetable broth

1 russet potato, skin on, cut into ½-inch (1 cm) cubes

1 cup (164 g) frozen or fresh corn

1 head broccoli (about 3 cups [200 g]), cut into tiny florets

2 cans (15 ounces [425 g]) brown lentils, drained and rinsed

1 can (14.5 ounces [411 g]) diced tomatoes, with juices

1½ cups (100 g) kale, roughly chopped into small pieces

1 teaspoon dried oregano

1 teaspoon sea salt

½ teaspoon black pepper

In a large stockpot, heat the oil over medium heat. Add the onion, celery, and carrots. Sauté for 3 minutes, until the onions are soft. Add the garlic and sauté for 1 minute, until fragrant.

Add the broth and potato, cover, and bring to a boil. Reduce to a simmer and continue to cook, covered, for 6 to 8 minutes, until the potatoes are fork-tender. Add the corn, broccoli, lentils, tomatoes, kale, oregano, salt, and pepper. Let simmer for 2 to 4 minutes, covered until the broccoli has become fork-tender.

Note

If you prefer dried lentils to canned lentils, simply cook them according to the package directions. Then add 1½ cups (297 g) cooked lentils in place of the canned.

Creamy Chickpea Potpie Soup

YIELD: 6 SERVINGS

Potpies are awesome: flaky crust bursting with creamy filling and delicious vegetables. But flaky store-bought vegan pastry crust is not yet always easy to come by. It never hurt nobody to cut some carbs from their dinner, so I put together this soup so I could have the nostalgic savory flavors served up in a flash in the convenience of a bowl. No baking required.

2 tablespoons (30 ml) olive oil (optional)

1 onion, chopped

2 carrots, thinly sliced

2 celery ribs, thinly sliced

4 cloves garlic, minced

2 russet potatoes, skin on and diced small

5 cups (1.2 L) vegetable broth, divided

1 cup (137 g) raw cashews, soaked in water overnight or boiled for 10 minutes in water and drained

1½ teaspoons poultry seasoning

1½ teaspoons sea salt, plus more for seasoning

1 cup (150 g) frozen peas

1 cup (164 g) frozen corn

1 can (15 ounces [425 g]) chickpeas, drained and rinsed

1 teaspoon black pepper, plus more for seasoning

1 tablespoon (15 ml) apple cider vinegar

Scallions or chives, roughly chopped (optional)

Heat the oil (if using) in a stockpot over medium heat. Add the onion, carrots, and celery and sauté for 3 to 5 minutes, until the onions are soft and translucent. Add the garlic and sauté for 1 minute, until fragrant.

Add the potatoes and 4 cups (940 ml) of broth to the pot. Cover and bring to a boil. Reduce to a simmer and cook, covered, for 8 to 10 minutes, until the potatoes are just fork-tender. Be careful not to let them turn to mush.

While soup is simmering, add the remaining broth, cashews, poultry seasoning, and salt to a blender. Blend for 1 to 2 minutes, until smooth and creamy. Transfer cream to the pot.

Add the peas, corn, chickpeas, pepper, and vinegar to the pot and stir until well combined. Bring to a simmer for 4 minutes to heat everything throughout. Season with salt and pepper to taste.

Serve hot garnished with scallions (if using).

Note

If managing a nut allergy, omit the cashews. Add ¼ cup (32 g) cornstarch to the blender in place of the cashews and blend as directed. Use this as the cream. After adding to the pot, let simmer 4 to 6 minutes, until slightly thicker. This won't be as creamy as the cashew cream, but it will still give you a luscious and silky texture.

Simple Seitan Tikka Masala

YIELD: 6 TO 8 SERVINGS

I started making this recipe several years ago. Since then, it has gone through many incarnations from just chickpeas to just seitan to using chicken meat alternative. I've settled on this combination of savory, succulent seitan paired with burst-in-your-mouth chickpea goodness. Upton's Naturals is my favorite brand when it comes to store-bought seitan. Housed in a luscious coconut cream sauce, it's become a "lick the bowl clean" sort of recipe in our home!

1 tablespoon (15 ml) olive oil

1 white onion, diced

3 cloves garlic, minced

1½ cups (352 g) seitan, roughly chopped into bite-size pieces

1 can (15 ounces [425 g]) chickpeas, drained and rinsed

¾ teaspoon sea salt

1 teaspoon ginger powder

1 teaspoon ground cumin

2 teaspoons (4 g) garam masala

2 tablespoons (32 g) tomato paste

1 can (14.5 ounces [411 g]) diced tomatoes, with juices

1 can (13.5 ounces [983 ml]) full-fat coconut milk

Cauliflower rice

Chopped fresh cilantro (optional)

Heat the oil in a large, deep skillet over medium heat. Add the onion and sauté for 3 minutes, until soft. Add the garlic and sauté for 1 minute, until fragrant. Add the seitan and chickpeas and let cook for 2 to 4 minutes to lightly sear the seitan.

Add the salt, ginger, cumin, and masala, and mix until well combined. Add the tomato paste, tomatoes, and coconut milk. Mix until well combined and bring to a simmer for 4 to 6 minutes, until heated through.

Serve over rice or cauliflower rice sprinkled with fresh cilantro (if using).

Roasted Cauliflower Tomato Soup

YIELD: 4 SERVINGS

This soup is the perfect winter weekday meal! Roasting the cauliflower adds a little more depth of flavor to this severely underrated vegetable, while the chickpeas fill you up and the chard offers its deep green veggie nutrients.

PLANT-BASED SIMPLE

2 pounds (910 g) cauliflower florets

1½ teaspoons olive oil

¼ teaspoon sea salt

Pinch of black pepper

2 cups (475 ml) gluten-free vegetable broth

1 cup (160 g) diced white onion

1 can (14.5 ounces [410 g]) organic tomato sauce

1 can (14.5 ounces [411 g]) organic diced tomatoes

1 can (15 ounces [425 g]) chickpeas, rinsed and drained

2 cups (72 g) loosely packed chopped Swiss chard

1 teaspoon dried Italian seasoning

¼ teaspoon crushed red pepper flakes

Salt and black pepper, to taste

Preheat your oven to 375°F (190°C, or gas mark 5) and line a baking sheet with parchment paper.

Toss the cauliflower florets together with the olive oil, salt, and pepper until evenly coated. Spread out on the baking sheet and roast for 30 minutes. Stir the florets halfway through the cooking time to promote even browning.

While the cauliflower is roasting, warm ¼ cup (60 ml) of the vegetable broth over medium heat in a large pot. Once hot, add the onions to the pot and sauté until translucent, about 3 to 5 minutes. Next, add the remainder of the vegetable broth, the tomato sauce, diced tomatoes, and chickpeas.

Bring the mixture to a boil and then lower the heat to a simmer. Add the Swiss chard, Italian seasoning, and red pepper flakes to the soup. Carefully add the roasted cauliflower to the soup, stirring it in slowly. Cover the pot with a lid and simmer for 5 minutes longer. Season with salt and pepper. Serve hot.

Note

To add more body to this soup, stir in 1 cup (185 g) cooked quinoa along with the roasted cauliflower.

Smoky Corn Chowder Bread Bowl

YIELD: 4 SERVINGS

Chowders are among the most comforting foods out there, and corn chowders in particular have always had a special place in my heart. I also am a huge fan of carbs, so this is a recipe consisting of smoky, creamy carbs inside a bowl made of toasty carbs. Luckily, for both you and me, this recipe is not made with heavy cream and instead takes advantage of the inherent starchiness of corn to thicken it.

1 teaspoon sunflower oil

2 shallots, diced

1 clove garlic, minced

4 cups (616 g) fresh corn kernels (or thawed frozen corn)

¼ cup (15 g) nutritional yeast

1 tablespoon (15 ml) liquid aminos

1 teaspoon liquid smoke

¾ teaspoon smoked paprika, plus more for garnish

½ teaspoon onion powder

1½ cups (355 ml) vegetable broth

1 cup (235 ml) unsweetened, nut-free nondairy milk

2 cups (60 g) packed baby spinach

2 tablespoons (5 g) chiffonade-cut fresh basil, plus more for garnish

4 sourdough bread bowls (8 ounces [225 g] each)

½ teaspoon salt, or to taste

Black pepper, to taste

In a large pot over medium heat, heat the sunflower oil. Add the shallots and garlic to the pot and sauté for 2 to 3 minutes. Add the corn kernels, nutritional yeast, liquid aminos, liquid smoke, smoked paprika, and onion powder to the pot and stir until combined.

Add the vegetable broth and nondairy milk to the corn mixture and bring to a boil. Reduce the heat to medium-low and carefully use an immersion blender to puree about half of the corn kernels (so the mixture remains slightly chunky).

Cover the pot, bring the soup to a simmer, and cook for 10 minutes, stirring occasionally. Fold the spinach and basil into the soup and cook for another 5 minutes. Meanwhile, preheat the oven to 300°F (150°C, or gas mark 2). Cut the tops out of the bread bowl loaves and cut the bread out of the center, leaving a roughly 1-inch (2.5 cm)-thick wall on all sides. Toast the loaves until lightly golden.

Season the soup with salt and pepper to taste and divide it among the bread bowls. Garnish with a sprinkle of smoked paprika and chiffonade-cut basil and serve immediately.

Note

If you do not have an immersion blender, you can transfer half of the soup to a blender in small batches and carefully puree it with a towel over the top instead of the lid (or else you run the risk of it exploding everywhere).

White Bean Garlic Bisque

YIELD: 2 SERVINGS

If you need a luxurious soup that is incredibly easy to whip up but is perfect for a classy dinner, you've found it right here. Creamy and bold with roasted garlic flavor, and protein-packed to boot, this bisque is sure to impress.

FOR THE SOUP

1 head garlic

Olive oil, for drizzling

1 cup (235 ml) gluten-free vegetable broth

1 can (15 ounces [425 g]) white beans, such as great northern, navy, or cannellini, rinsed and drained

¼ cup (35 g) pine nuts

½ cup (115 ml) unsweetened soy-free nondairy milk

½ teaspoon salt

⅛ teaspoon freshly ground white pepper

Pinch of ground nutmeg

FOR THE GARNISH

Garlic olive oil, for drizzling

8 sprigs of fresh thyme or oregano

2 tablespoons (18 g) pine nuts, toasted

Preheat the oven to 350°F (180°C, or gas mark 4).

Cut off the top ½ inch (1.3 cm) of the head of garlic, exposing a little of each clove, and then coat the tops with a thin layer of olive oil. Wrap the entire head in aluminum foil, place it on a small baking sheet, and roast for 30 to 45 minutes until the cloves are soft.

Let the garlic cool until you can handle it and then peel off the foil and squeeze the soft garlic out of the peels and into a blender. Add the remaining soup ingredients to the blender, puree until very smooth, and transfer to a pot.

Warm the soup over medium heat until it starts to simmer and then simmer for 5 to 10 minutes, stirring occasionally. Divide soup between 2 bowls. Garnish with a light drizzle of garlic olive oil, sprigs of thyme, and toasted pine nuts. Serve immediately.

Notes

If you prefer, you can use soaked and drained raw cashews or silken tofu in the soup instead of the pine nuts. Note that this recipe will not be soy-free if tofu is added.

To make garlic oil, place 8 cloves garlic and ½ cup (115 ml) olive oil in a small saucepan over medium-low heat and cook for 5 minutes to infuse the oil. Strain the oil, transfer to a sealable bottle or jar, and refrigerate.

Mushroom Wild Rice
Slow Cooker Stew

YIELD: 4 SERVINGS

Slow cookers are a highly underutilized appliance, in my opinion. So to help win over any skeptics, here is a hearty stew of mixed mushrooms, wild rice, filling black lentils, and fresh herbs that will have you set for dinner without putting too much effort into it.

1 tablespoon (15 ml) sunflower oil

1½ cups (240 g) diced white onion

½ pound (225 g) baby bella mushrooms, sliced

1 ounce (28 g) dried porcini mushrooms, chopped

1 cup (192 g) black lentils

1 cup (160 g) wild rice

1 tablespoon (3 g) chopped fresh sage leaves

4 sprigs of fresh thyme

3 sprigs of fresh rosemary, plus more for garnish

7 cups (1.6 L) gluten-free, soy-free vegetable broth

3 cups (710 ml) water

2 teaspoons salt

1 teaspoon black pepper

In a small pan, heat the sunflower oil over medium heat. Add the onions and baby bella mushrooms and sauté for 3 to 5 minutes until the onions become translucent and the mushrooms have reduced in size.

Place the onion-mushroom mixture in a 4-quart (3.8 L) slow cooker, along with the dried porcini mushrooms, lentils, rice, sage, thyme, and rosemary. Toss the ingredients together and then cover with the vegetable broth and water. Cover with the lid and cook for 7 to 8 hours on high, stirring occasionally.

Before serving, stir in the salt and pepper and pick out the thyme and rosemary stems if possible.

Garnish each bowl with 1 or 2 sprigs of rosemary and serve.

Note

Check the label on the wild rice package to make sure it is soy-free.

Mean Green Ramen

YIELD: 4 SERVINGS

For the first part of my adult life, ramen was something that was eaten out of a plastic cup, when you were busy spending all your money on school supplies and beer. (I'm talking college here.) I've been lucky enough to experience traditional ramen since then, and though there are a few different types, here I give you a miso-based broth version loaded up with green veggies.

2 teaspoons untoasted sesame oil

2 tablespoons (16 g) grated fresh ginger

6 cloves garlic, minced

8 cups (1.9 L) water

2 cups (475 ml) vegetable broth

¼ cup (60 ml) soy sauce

1 teaspoon dulse seaweed granules

¼ cup (63 g) yellow miso paste

8 ounces (225 g) ramen noodles (also called chuka soba)

2 heads baby bok choy, quartered

2 cups (142 g) broccoli florets

1 package (14 ounces [390 g]) firm tofu, cubed

3½ ounces (100 g) maitake mushrooms, broken into smaller pieces

2 sheets of nori seaweed, cut into strips

1 cup (104 g) mung bean sprouts

Chili-sesame oil, for drizzling (optional)

Heat the sesame oil in a large soup pot over medium heat. Add the ginger and garlic and sauté for 2 minutes. Add the water, vegetable broth, soy sauce, and dulse granules to the pot and bring to a boil.

Add the miso paste and ramen noodles to the boiling water and cook the noodles according to the package instructions. For the last 2 to 3 minutes of the cooking time, add the bok choy, broccoli, tofu, and mushrooms to the pot.

Stir the soup, making sure the miso paste has fully dissolved. Remove from the heat and carefully divide the ramen among 4 large soup bowls. Top each bowl with a few strips of nori, ¼ cup (26 g) mung bean sprouts, and a drizzle of chili-sesame oil, if using. Serve hot.

Note

Dulse is a type of seaweed. Dried granules and flakes can be found at some well-stocked grocery stores or online.

Sick Day Veggie Noodle Soup

YIELD: 6 SERVINGS

This simple vegetable soup is just what you need when you are feeling under the weather and want to get something warm, delicious, and nurturing into your system. Brussels sprouts, carrots, zucchini, and celeriac (one of my favorite root vegetables) provide nutritious substance to the seasoned broth and noodles.

PLANT-BASED SIMPLE

2 teaspoons olive oil

1 cup (160 g) diced white onion

1 pound (455 g) Brussels sprouts, trimmed and thinly sliced lengthwise

½ pound (225 g) celeriac, peeled and diced

¼ pound (115 g) rainbow carrots, sliced into coins

½ pound (225 g) zucchini, quartered lengthwise, then sliced

8 cups (1.9 L) vegetable broth

1½ teaspoons poultry seasoning (gluten-free, if necessary)

4 ounces (115 g) angel hair pasta, broken up into 1-inch (2.5 cm) pieces (gluten-free, if necessary)

1 teaspoon salt, or to taste

¼ teaspoon black pepper

Heat the olive oil in a large pot over medium heat. Sauté the onion, Brussels sprouts, celeriac, and carrots until the onions are translucent. Add the zucchini to the pot, sauté for 5 more minutes, and then add the vegetable broth and poultry seasoning. Bring the soup to a boil.

Add the angel hair pasta pieces, cover, and cook for 10 minutes or until the noodles are soft. Stir in the salt and pepper and serve.

Sweet Potato Eggplant Curry

YIELD: 4 SERVINGS

I did not try eating curries until after college, but ever since my first bite I have been hooked. Green, red, yellow: You name it, I love it. Here we have a yellow curry with sweet potatoes, eggplant, tofu, and jasmine rice. There are so many flavors and enticing aromas!

1 package (12 ounces [340 g]) extra-firm tofu, rinsed and drained

1 tablespoon (14 g) coconut oil

1 cup (160 g) chopped red onion

1 tablespoon (6 g) minced lemongrass

1 tablespoon (6 g) minced fresh ginger

1¼ pounds (570 g) sweet potatoes, peeled and chopped

¾ pound (340 g) eggplant, peeled and chopped

3 tablespoons (19 g) yellow curry powder

1 can (13.5 ounces [400 ml]) full-fat coconut milk

5 cups (1.2 L) gluten-free vegetable broth

½ cup (92 g) jasmine rice

2 tablespoons (28 ml) lime juice

1½ teaspoons salt

¼ cup (15 g) unsweetened coconut flakes, toasted

1 teaspoon lime zest

Wrap the tofu tightly in a clean kitchen towel, set on a plate, and place a couple of weights on top of it to press out some of the moisture. In a large pot over medium heat, melt the coconut oil and sauté the red onion, lemongrass, and ginger until the onions are translucent.

Unwrap the tofu and cut into small cubes; add the sweet potatoes and tofu to the pot and sauté for 5 to 7 minutes until the sides of the tofu are golden. Add the eggplant and curry powder to the pot and sauté for 2 minutes. Add the coconut milk and vegetable broth and bring the curry to a boil.

Add the jasmine rice, reduce the heat to medium-low, cover, and cook for 15 to 20 minutes until the water is absorbed and the rice is cooked.

Stir in the lime juice and salt. Divide the curry among 4 bowls and top each one with toasted coconut and lime zest, and serve.

Pumpkin Chickpea Chili

YIELD: 10 SERVINGS

I came up with this dish years ago during my yearly autumn obsession with pumpkins. It has become a simple dinner recipe that I enjoy serving just about any time of year, although we particularly enjoy it on brisk autumn nights.

1 onion, diced

2 cloves garlic, minced

½ green bell pepper, diced

½ to 1 teaspoon salt

1 tablespoon (15 ml) olive oil

1 cup (130 g) frozen or fresh corn

1 can (28 ounces [793 g]) diced tomatoes

1 can (15 ounces [420 g]) pumpkin puree

1 can (15 ounces [420 g]) chickpeas, drained and rinsed

1 can (15 ounces [420 g]) black beans, drained and rinsed

1 to 3 teaspoons chili powder, to taste

2 teaspoons cumin

1 cup (235 ml) vegetable broth

Zest and juice of 1 lime

Black pepper, to taste

¼ to ½ cup (4 to 8 g) minced cilantro, for garnish

In a large skillet over medium heat, sauté the onion, garlic, green pepper, and salt in olive oil for 10 to 15 minutes or until tender. Stir in the remaining ingredients, increase the heat to high, and bring to a boil. Immediately reduce the heat to medium-low and simmer for 15 to 20 minutes until heated through. Garnish with fresh cilantro and serve hot.

Note

Variations of this chili can be created by using different types of winter squash in place of pumpkin. Roasted and pureed acorn, butternut, or delicata varieties work well.

Coconut Asparagus Soup

YIELD: 4 APPETIZER-SIZE SERVINGS

Two of my favorite foods come together beautifully in this dish. The desiccated coconut adds a hint of texture to the pureed soup, and the asparagus incorporates a deep flavor and richness without the need for a cream base.

About 25 thin stalks asparagus, tough ends removed

1 small sweet onion, chopped (about 1 cup [160 g])

⅓ cup (30 g) desiccated coconut (unsweetened), soaked overnight and then drained

2 tablespoons (30 ml) extra-virgin olive oil, plus more for drizzling

⅔ cup (160 ml) water

Salt, to taste

2 cups (470 ml) nondairy milk or vegetable broth

Steam the asparagus until tender, 5 to 7 minutes.

Meanwhile, combine the onion, coconut, 2 tablespoons (30 ml) olive oil, and water in a shallow pan and cook over medium-high heat until the onion is tender and all the water has been absorbed, stirring often to prevent sticking, about 10 minutes. Lightly season with salt.

Chill both the steamed asparagus and the cooked onion just until cold enough to place in a blender, about 15 minutes. Chop the asparagus into bite-size pieces.

Transfer the veggies, reserving about ½ cup (50 g) of the asparagus for garnishing the soup, and the nondairy milk to a blender and blend until smooth, about 5 minutes. Add salt to taste.

Reheat on the stovetop to the desired temperature. Garnish with a drizzle of olive oil and the reserved asparagus.

Minted Green Pea Bisque

YIELD: 2 SERVINGS

This recipe is extremely easy to make and is always a welcome addition to almost any meal. Served hot or cold, it makes an equally perfect soup for a chilly winter night or a warm summer day.

1 small sweet onion, minced

1 clove garlic, minced

2 tablespoons (30 ml) water

1 teaspoon sea salt, divided

3 cups (450 g) frozen or fresh green peas

2 tablespoons (12 g) minced fresh mint leaves

1 cup (235 ml) nondairy milk, plus more if needed

Fresh cracked black pepper, to taste

In a small frying pan over medium-high heat, sauté the onion and garlic in the water until translucent. Season with ¼ teaspoon of the salt. Reduce the heat to medium-low and simmer until the onions are caramelized, about 10 minutes. Remove from the heat and let cool.

Bring a medium-size pot of water to a boil, and then add the peas and cook until tender, about 5 minutes if frozen or 2 to 3 minutes if fresh. Drain well and then rinse under cold water until the peas are cool to the touch.

Transfer the peas to a blender and add the sautéed onions and garlic, mint leaves, nondairy milk, and remaining ¾ teaspoon salt. Blend for 5 minutes or until super smooth. Add more nondairy milk if the soup seems too thick for your taste.

Warm gently over medium heat, sprinkle with pepper, and serve.

Fajita Soup

YIELD: 6 SERVINGS

My favorite part of this soup is the smokiness of the broth in contrast to the bright and colorful veggies. Topping with sliced avocados right before serving adds a little creaminess to this brothy vegetable soup.

½ cup (75 g) stemmed, seeded, and chopped red bell pepper

½ cup (75 g) stemmed, seeded, and chopped yellow bell pepper

½ cup (75 g) stemmed, seeded, and chopped orange bell pepper

2 cups (240 g) chopped zucchini

1 small red onion, thinly sliced

6 cremini or button mushrooms, sliced (about 1 cup [70 g])

2 tablespoons (30 ml) olive oil

1 can (15 ounces [420 g]) black beans, drained and rinsed

1 can (28 ounces [794 g]) diced tomatoes

6 cups (1,410 ml) vegetable broth

2 teaspoons cumin

½ teaspoon chipotle chili powder

2 tablespoons (30 ml) fresh lime juice, plus extra for serving

Salt, to taste

2 ripe avocados, chopped, for garnish

Heat a large frying pan over medium heat just until hot. Toss in the peppers, zucchini, onion, mushrooms, and oil and sauté over medium-high heat until the vegetables are tender, 10 to 15 minutes, stirring often to prevent sticking.

Transfer the cooked vegetables to a large soup pot and stir in the black beans, diced tomatoes, vegetable broth, cumin, chili powder, and 2 tablespoons (30 ml) lime juice. Add salt to taste. Simmer for about 15 minutes until heated through.

Garnish with the avocado and a squeeze of lime juice and serve.

Smoky Sweet Potato Soup

YIELD: 5 SERVINGS

When I first went vegan, I subscribed to a Community Supported Agriculture (CSA) box, and the company that ran it would send recipe suggestions with each delivery. This played a huge part in my learning how to cook! A recipe similar to this one came to me with a ton of sweet potatoes, and after some serious tweaking I think it has reached its full potential. Smoky but not overly so, a little sweet but still savory, and super-satiating. Though the toasted bread is optional, I love eating this soup with a crusty slice of sourdough.

1 tablespoon (15 ml) sunflower oil

1½ cups (190 g) diced red onion

1¼ cups (188 g) diced orange bell pepper

1½ pounds (680 g) sweet potatoes, unpeeled, diced

2 large carrots, chopped

3 cloves garlic, minced

2 tablespoons (10 g) nutritional yeast

2 teaspoons (5 g) smoked paprika

1 teaspoon garlic powder

1 teaspoon ground cumin

4 cups (950 ml) vegetable broth

2 cups (475 ml) water

⅔ cup (116 g) red quinoa, rinsed

1 cup (110 g) frozen spinach, broken up into pieces

½–1 teaspoon salt

½ cup (70 g) roasted pumpkin seeds (pepitas)

¼ cup (4 g) fresh cilantro leaves

5 slices of toasted crusty bread (optional)

In a large pot, heat the sunflower oil over medium heat. Add the red onion and bell pepper and cook, stirring frequently, until the onion is softened, about 5 minutes. Adjust the heat to medium-low and add the sweet potatoes, carrots, garlic, nutritional yeast, smoked paprika, garlic powder, and cumin. Cook for 5 more minutes, adding 1 or 2 tablespoons (15 to 30 ml) water if necessary to prevent sticking.

Stir in the vegetable broth, water, and quinoa, cover, and bring to a boil over medium-high heat. Once boiling, adjust the heat so that the soup is simmering, cover, and cook, stirring occasionally, until the quinoa is tender, about 20 minutes longer.

Puree half of the soup mixture using an immersion blender or by carefully transferring to a blender. Add the spinach, stirring to break up any clumps, and add salt to taste. Let the soup cool for 20 minutes, then divide it between 5 jars or storage containers. Top each serving with the pumpkin seeds and cilantro and store in the refrigerator for up to 7 days. Serve with a slice of bread, if desired.

Note

This soup is great for storing in the fridge to eat during the week, and it also freezes well if you want to plan way ahead. If you choose to freeze it, divide it into five freezer-safe storage containers and freeze for up to 6 months.

Grilled Gazpacho Verde

YIELD: 4 SERVINGS

I've made plenty of tomato-based gazpachos, which are an excellent way to use up that summer garden bounty. However, this green version is definitely my new favorite, because of its added grilled flavor and refreshing toppings!

FOR THE GAZPACHO

3 poblano or Anaheim peppers

1 jalapeño

1 pound (455 g) tomatillos with husks removed

1 red onion, sliced in half

1 cup (235 ml) water

1 cup (120 g) corn kernels

½ cup (68 g) raw cashews

¼ cup (8 g) loosely packed cilantro

2 tablespoons (30 ml) lime juice

1 clove garlic

Salt

FOR THE TOPPING

1½ cups (205 g) diced cucumbers

1 cup (120 g) corn kernels

1 cup (135 g) diced avocado

2 tablespoons (5 g) minced cilantro

1 tablespoon (15 ml) lime juice

¼ teaspoon salt

⅛ teaspoon black pepper

To make the gazpacho

Using a grill or grill pan, carefully char the poblanos and jalapeño until the skins are nearly black, then place them in a bowl and cover it so the peppers can steam. Grill the tomatillos and red onion until they have softened slightly and have bold, visible grill marks. Uncover the bowl and carefully scrape the charred skin from the peppers using a butter knife. Stem and seed the peppers and transfer them to a large blender pitcher.

Cut the tomatillos into quarters and cut the red onion pieces in half, then add them to the blender along with the water, corn, and cashews. Blend until the mixture is very smooth, then let it settle for 5 minutes before adding the cilantro, lime juice, and garlic and blending again until very smooth. (If your blender is on the smaller side, you may need to do this in batches.) Season with salt to taste, then divide the gazpacho between 4 bowls or storage containers and refrigerate while you assemble the topping.

To make the topping

Combine the cucumbers, corn, avocado, cilantro, lime juice, salt, and pepper in a small bowl. Once the gazpacho is thoroughly chilled, top each serving with some of the salsa. The topped gazpacho can be stored in the refrigerator for up to 5 days.

Hawaiian Tofu and Pineapple Sando

YIELD: 4 SANDWICHES

This tofu has that succulent balance of smoky and sweet. It's topped with a super simple slaw with some pineapple chunks for a touch of tang. Colorful, flavorful, and easy to pull together, this is a great sandwich for any day of the week. If you can't find, or don't like ciabatta, use your bread bun or roll of choice.

FOR THE TOFU

2 tablespoons (30 ml) olive oil

2 tablespoons (28 ml) soy sauce or gluten-free tamari

1 tablespoon (15 g) Dijon mustard

¼ cup (38 g) dark brown sugar

1 teaspoon smoked paprika

2 teaspoons (5 g) garlic powder

2 teaspoons (5 g) onion powder

½ teaspoon sea salt

¼ teaspoon black pepper

1 package (14 ounces [396 g]) extra-firm tofu, cut into 12 slices

4 vegan ciabatta rolls

FOR THE PINEAPPLE SLAW

½ cup (85 g) fresh or canned pineapple chunks, drained

1 cup (70 g) shredded red cabbage

¼ cup (60 g) vegan mayonnaise

½ teaspoon apple cider vinegar

2 pinches sea salt

Preheat the oven to 425°F (220°C, or gas mark 7). Line a sheet pan with parchment paper.

To make the tofu
Combine the olive oil, soy sauce, Dijon mustard, brown sugar, smoked paprika, garlic powder, onion powder, salt, and pepper in a bowl. Lay the slices of tofu out on the prepared sheet pan in one layer and brush each slice of tofu with the mixture. Half of the mixture should remain after brushing one side. If you don't have a pastry brush, use a paper towel to dab the mixture onto the pieces of tofu. Bake for 15 minutes. Remove from the oven, flip, and brush the other side. Bake for 15 minutes, or until darker brown.

To make the pineapple slaw
While the tofu finishes baking, combine the pineapple, cabbage, mayonnaise, vinegar, and salt in a small bowl. Mix until well combined.

Remove the tofu from the sheet pan. Place 3 slices on the bottom roll and top with one-quarter of the slaw mixture; continue with remaining ciabatta rolls.

Note

Toast that bread to take this sandwich to the next level. Spread the inside of the top and bottom of the ciabatta roll with vegan butter and grill face down on a skillet until light brown and toasted.

Mushroom Carnitas and Brussels Burrito with Sweet Red Onion

YIELD: 2 BURRITOS

Mushrooms: If you like them (and I do), you know they are magical. Not that kind of magical (get your head out of the gutter). They take on such a rich and deep flavor when tossed with some oil and roasted in the oven, and they make anything they are added to nice and hearty. With the texture of Brussels sprouts and chickpeas and the sweet hint of maple-kissed red onions, this is a very satisfying burrito.

5 ounces (140 g) sliced shiitake mushrooms

1½ cups (135 g) Brussels sprouts, trimmed and roughly chopped

½ cup (120 g) chickpeas, drained and rinsed

2 tablespoons (15 ml) olive oil, divided

½ teaspoon sea salt

¼ teaspoon black pepper

½ red onion, thinly sliced

2 teaspoons (14 g) maple syrup

2 large (10-inch [26 cm]) burrito flour tortillas

Vegan sour cream

Sriracha (optional)

Preheat the oven to 400°F (200°C, or gas mark 6). Line a sheet pan with parchment paper.

Add the mushrooms, Brussels sprouts, and chickpeas to one side of the sheet pan. Drizzle with 1 tablespoon (15 ml) olive oil, and sprinkle with salt and pepper. Toss well to combine. Add the onion to the other side of the sheet pan, drizzle with the remaining olive oil, and toss to combine. Bake for 15 minutes and flip the mushroom mixture. Add the maple syrup to the onion and toss to combine. Bake for 15 minutes, until the mushrooms have browned and reduced in size. Remove from the oven and toss everything with a spatula to mix the onions into the mushroom mixture until combined.

Divide the mixture among the 2 tortillas, add sour cream, and drizzle with sriracha (if using). Fold the side of the tortilla closest to you over the filling, then tuck in both sides and roll the burrito away from you until completely wrapped.

Note

The tighter the roll, the more intact the ingredients will stay, meaning a less sloppy eating experience. YouTube has great videos for getting your wrap or burrito roll game on right and tight.

Breezy Cauliflower and Chorizo Brunch Tacos

YIELD: 6 TACOS

This cauliflower sort-of-scramble is a great option if you either don't like tofu or are just plum sick and tired of tofu scrambles. Zesty chorizo flavors bring this home when topped with salsa, sour cream, and scallions. Be sure to roughly chop the cauliflower florets into small chunks to resemble more of a scramble.

2 cups (264 g) roughly chopped cauliflower florets

½ cup (80 g) roughly chopped red onion

1 tablespoon (15 ml) olive oil

2 tablespoons (10 g) nutritional yeast

½ teaspoon ground cumin

½ teaspoon ground turmeric

½ teaspoon Himalayan black salt (kala namak) (optional)

1½ cups (152 g) vegan chorizo or sausage, crumbled or roughly chopped

6 (6-inch [15 cm]) corn tortillas, hard or soft

6 tablespoons (98 g) store-bought salsa

2 tablespoons (28 g) vegan sour cream

4 scallions, thinly sliced (optional)

Preheat the oven to 425°F (220°C, or gas mark 7). Line a large sheet pan with parchment paper.

Add the cauliflower florets and red onion to the sheet pan. Drizzle with the olive oil and sprinkle with nutritional yeast, cumin, turmeric, and black salt. Toss until well combined and the cauliflower has taken on a yellow hue from the turmeric. Bake for 15 minutes, until the cauliflower has reduced slightly in size.

Add the chorizo to the sheet pan and toss until well combined. Bake for 15 minutes, until the cauliflower is slightly charred. Add the tortillas to the top of the mixture, overlapping each other if needed, and let warm in the oven for 2 minutes.

Remove from the oven and build each taco by dividing the mixture among the tortillas. Add salsa and sour cream to each taco, and sprinkle with scallions (if using).

Note

Serve mini tacos as an appetizer at your brunch to get guests talking about how much of a genius you are. You can't help it—you're amazing. To pump up the serving style, cut the edge off the long side of a lime so it sits flat on a surface and then cut one wedge out of the opposite side big enough for a mini taco to sit in. A mini taco sitting in a lime wedge: Lookatchu and your catering skills. It's a super fun serving option for brunch. Pro tip: Mini shells are available for purchase on the interwebs.

Curried Tofu Wraps

YIELD: 5 SERVINGS

These tofu wraps are like a tornado of flavors, colors, and textures! Firm, baked tofu combined with a creamy tahini sauce and crunchy veggies make these wraps simple, but oh so delicious.

FOR THE TOFU

2 packages (14 ounces [397 g]) firm tofu, drained and rinsed

Cooking spray

1½ tablespoons (10 g) yellow curry powder

2 teaspoons (5 g) onion powder

½ teaspoon salt

½ teaspoon black pepper

FOR THE COCONUT-TAHINI SAUCE

½ cup (120 ml) full-fat coconut milk, stirred well

⅓ cup (80 g) tahini

3 tablespoons (45 ml) lime juice

¼ teaspoon salt

FOR THE ASSEMBLY

5 burrito-sized flour tortillas or 10 small gluten-free wraps

2½ cups (225 g) shredded red cabbage

2 red or orange bell peppers, stemmed, seeded, and sliced into strips

½ cup (840 g) thinly sliced red onion

¼ cup (4 g) loosely packed fresh cilantro

To make the tofu

Preheat the oven to 400°F (200°C, or gas mark 6) and line a baking sheet with parchment paper. Wrap the tofu in a kitchen towel or paper towels, place something heavy on top of it (books or large cans work well), and let it drain while the oven preheats.

Slice each block of tofu into ½-inch (1 cm)-thick slabs. Place them on the baking sheet in a single layer and lightly coat with cooking spray. In a small bowl, whisk together the curry powder, onion powder, salt, and pepper. Sprinkle half of the spice mix over one side of the tofu and bake for 15 minutes. Flip the tofu, lightly coat with cooking spray, and sprinkle on the remaining spice mix. Bake for an additional 15 minutes.

To make the coconut-tahini sauce

While the tofu is baking, whisk the coconut milk, tahini, lime juice, and salt in a small bowl. Refrigerate the sauce until you're ready to assemble the wraps.

To assemble

Divide the coconut-tahini sauce among the wraps, spreading it over the center of each tortilla. Next, place the cabbage, bell pepper, onion, cilantro, and tofu on top of the sauce. Working with 1 tortilla at a time, wrap up the tortilla by folding 2 sides of the tortilla toward the center, then rolling the unfolded end closest to you over the filling. Keep rolling until the wrap is completely closed. Serve immediately or store in the refrigerator, wrapped in foil or in an airtight container, for up to 5 days.

Note

Make sure that your coconut milk is completely emulsified, or your sauce may be too thin or too thick.

Peanutty Tempeh Banh Mi

YIELD: 5 SERVINGS

There's a huge Vietnamese population in the county where I've spent most of my life, and I'm lucky to have eaten so much Vietnamese food over the years. One tried-and-true dish that I'll order almost any time I see it on a menu is banh mi. Pickled veggies, fresh herbs, spicy jalapeños, and a savory, protein-rich filling? Yes, please!

FOR THE VEGGIES

2 tablespoons (30 ml) unseasoned rice vinegar

2 teaspoons (10 ml) agave nectar

¼ teaspoon salt

1 cup (116 g) peeled and thinly sliced daikon radish

1 cup (119 g) peeled and thinly sliced cucumber

1 cup (130 g) peeled and thinly sliced carrot

FOR THE TEMPEH

1 cup (235 ml) water

2 packages (8 ounces [225 g]) gluten-free tempeh

¼ cup (65 g) natural smooth peanut butter

2 tablespoons (30 ml) unseasoned rice vinegar

1½ tablespoons (25 ml) tamari

1 tablespoon (10 g) sambal oelek chili paste

1 tablespoon (15 ml) agave nectar

FOR THE ASSEMBLY

5 hoagie-style sandwich buns or 2 baguettes, gluten-free if desired

5 tablespoons (60 g) vegan mayo

¼ cup (4 g) cilantro leaves

¼ cup (6 g) basil or Thai basil leaves

1 small jalapeño, sliced (optional)

To make the veggies

In a medium bowl, whisk together the rice vinegar, agave, and salt. Add the daikon radish, cucumber, and carrot and toss until the veggies are coated. Refrigerate the mixture until you're ready to assemble the sandwiches.

To make the tempeh

In a large sauté pan, bring the water to a simmer over medium-low heat. Cut the tempeh into 8 equal slabs and place them in the simmering water. Cover the pan with a lid and simmer the tempeh for 5 minutes to get rid of its bitterness. Transfer the tempeh to a cutting board and slice it into ½-inch (1 cm) thick strips. Drain the water from the pan.

In a large bowl, whisk together the peanut butter, rice vinegar, tamari, chili paste, and agave nectar until smooth. Add the tempeh and toss gently to coat in sauce. Add half of the mixture to the now-empty pan and cook over medium-low heat until warmed through, about 5 minutes. Transfer the cooked tempeh to a bowl and repeat with the remaining tempeh mixture.

To assemble

Slice the rolls in half lengthwise, leaving 1 side uncut for a hinge. Spread each roll with 1 tablespoon of the mayo, then layer on the tempeh and pickled veggies. Divide the cilantro and basil evenly among the sandwiches. Serve immediately or store in the refrigerator, wrapped in foil or in an airtight container, for up to 5 days.

Note

If you can't find daikon radish, thinly sliced red radishes will also work, though they are a little more peppery.

Fajita Pita Pockets

YIELD: 5 SERVINGS

While these fajita pitas would be great as burritos or wraps, I love the ease of shoving all the delicious fillings into a pita pocket. This recipe comes together so quickly, you could make it on your lunch break!

1 tablespoon (15 ml) organic sunflower oil

2 red bell peppers, sliced into strips

2 green bell peppers, sliced into strips

1 cup (120 g) halved and sliced red onion

¼ teaspoon salt

2 cans (15 ounces [425 g]) vegan refried beans

1 teaspoon garlic powder

1 teaspoon ground cumin

5 pitas or gluten-free wraps if desired

5 cups (205 g) chopped romaine

1 avocado, sliced

5 lime wedges

In a large skillet, heat the oil over medium-high heat. Add the bell peppers and onion and cook until they have some brown edges but are not limp, 5 to 7 minutes. Season with salt to taste. While the peppers and onions are cooking, combine the refried beans, garlic powder, and cumin in a small skillet over medium-low heat and cook until they are warmed through. Set aside.

Toast or warm up the pitas to make them more pliable, if desired, then cut each of them in half. Spread the refried bean mixture onto 1 inner side of each pita half. Next, divide the pepper-onion mixture, romaine, and sliced avocado evenly among the pitas. Refrigerate the pita pockets, with a lime wedge on the side, in storage containers or bags for up to 7 days. If you prefer to eat them warm, keep the romaine and avocado on the side as you reheat the pocket.

Cajun Chickpea Salad Wraps

YIELD: 4 SERVINGS

Cool, creamy, crunchy, and with just the right amount of spice, these spicy chickpea salad wraps come together in no time at all and are a great lunch to bring with you to school or work. Honestly, the cashew sauce alone makes this worthwhile—make extra and put it on everything!

PLANT-BASED SIMPLE

2 cans (15 ounces [425 g]) chickpeas, drained, ⅔ cup (160 ml) liquid reserved

¾ cup (90 g) raw cashews

2 tablespoons (10 g) nutritional yeast

1 tablespoon (6 g) Cajun spice blend

1 tablespoon (15 ml) white vinegar

½ teaspoon agave nectar

½ teaspoon salt

1 cup (150 g) diced red bell pepper

1 cup (120 g) corn kernels

¼ cup (35 g) diced red onion

4 burrito-sized tortillas or 8 gluten-free wraps

8 leaves romaine, cut in half widthwise

Puree the reserved chickpea liquid, cashews, nutritional yeast, Cajun spice, vinegar, agave nectar, and salt in a blender until very smooth. Let sit for 5 minutes, then blend again until very smooth. Meanwhile, combine the chickpeas, bell pepper, corn, and red onion in a large bowl.

Pour the sauce over the chickpea mixture and stir to evenly coat everything. (The sauce may seem thin, but it will thicken as it chills.) Refrigerate the chickpea salad for 15 minutes, then stir well. Warm the tortillas in the microwave or one at a time over a gas stove burner until pliable. Place 4 pieces of romaine in the center of each tortilla and top with chickpea salad.

Working with one tortilla at a time, wrap up the tortilla by folding 2 sides of the tortilla toward the center, then rolling the unfolded end closest to you over the filling. Keep rolling until the wrap is completely closed. Serve right away, or store in the refrigerator in a lunch container or wrapped in foil for up to 5 days.

CHAPTER FOUR
Salads

Italian Cheesy Herbed Tofu and Kale Bowl

YIELD: 2 SERVINGS

This tofu is my absolute favorite to have on hand for meal prep. But I promise you, the leftover tofu from this recipe won't hang around long! Zesty from the lemon juice, herby from a blend of Italian seasoning, and salty and nutty from the nutritional yeast baked with a perfect crust, it's irresistible.

FOR THE ITALIAN CHEESY HERB TOFU

1 package (14 ounces [396 g]) extra-firm tofu, drained, cut into ½-inch (1 cm) cubes

1 tablespoon (15 ml) olive oil

Juice of ½ lemon

¼ cup (20 g) nutritional yeast

1½ teaspoons Italian seasoning

1 teaspoon onion powder

1 teaspoon sea salt

1 teaspoon garlic powder

½ teaspoon black pepper

FOR THE BOWL

4 cups (268 g) kale, stems removed and cut into bite-size pieces

2 teaspoons (10 ml) olive oil

½ cup (118 g) shredded carrot

1 avocado, peeled, and sliced

1 cup (198 g) canned lentils, drained

Vegan salad dressing

2 tablespoons (30 g) crushed pecans (optional)

2 tablespoons (12 g) thinly sliced scallions (optional)

Preheat the oven to 425°F (220°C, or gas mark 7). Line a sheet pan with parchment paper.

To make the Italian cheesy herb tofu
Combine the tofu, oil, lemon juice, nutritional yeast, Italian seasoning, onion powder, salt, garlic powder, and pepper in a bowl. Mix until combined and evenly coated. Transfer the mixture to the prepared sheet pan and bake for 10 minutes. Flip the tofu with a spatula and bake for 10 minutes, until darkened and slightly crisp. Remove from the oven and let cool.

To make the bowl
Divide the kale into 2 bowls and drizzle each with 1 teaspoon olive oil. Massage the kale until it is dark green and soft. Divide the carrot, avocado, and lentils between the 2 bowls and top with ¼ cup (30 g) baked tofu. Drizzle each bowl with dressing of choice, and sprinkle with pecans and scallions (if using).

Note

If you have an air fryer, toss this tofu together in a bowl and air-fry at 380°F (193°C) for 8 minutes. Toss and then continue air-frying at 380°F (193°C) for 8 minutes, until you have the perfect crispy outside with a little pillowy puff of tofu in the middle.

Good Goddess Choppy Salad

YIELD: 2 SALADS

Once upon a time, I waited tables at a restaurant in NYC where the chef created a new chopped salad every day. I came to LOVE this salad in particular and had it almost every shift for my meal. What I enjoyed the most was the simplicity of the ingredients. It had a lot of crunch with different textures and vibrant flavors from so many components being packed into one bowl!

SALADS

FOR THE GOOD GODDESS DRESSING

½ cup (120 g) tahini

¼ cup (59 ml) olive oil

¼ cup (60 ml) water, plus more as needed

2 tablespoons (28 ml) apple cider vinegar

2 tablespoons (28 ml) soy sauce or gluten-free tamari

Juice of 1 lemon

1 teaspoon garlic powder

½ teaspoon onion powder

½ teaspoon dried parsley

FOR THE CHOPPY SALAD

2 cups (110 g) romaine, roughly chopped

2 cups (60 g) baby spinach

1 cup (248 g) extra-firm tofu, drained and cut into ½-inch (1 cm) cubes

½ cup (75 g) grape tomatoes, halved

½ cup (135 g) roughly chopped cucumber

½ cup (118 g) shredded carrot

¼ cup (60 g) walnuts

1 apple (any variety), cored and roughly chopped

¼ cup (32 g) green olives, pitted

2 tablespoons (15 g) dried cranberries or cherries

1 teaspoon hemp seeds

To make the good goddess dressing

Add the tahini, olive oil, water, vinegar, soy sauce, lemon juice, garlic powder, and onion powder to a blender. Blend for 1 to 2 minutes, until smooth and creamy. Add more water as needed, 1 tablespoon (15 ml) at a time, to reach desired consistency.

Add the dried parsley to the blender and blend for 10 to 15 seconds, until evenly dispersed but specks are still visible.

To make the choppy salad

Lay the romaine and spinach on a cutting board and chop roughly with a knife until cut into bite-size pieces. Divide the spinach and lettuce mixture into 2 bowls. Lay the tofu, tomatoes, cucumber, carrot, walnuts, apple, and green olives on the same cutting board and chop everything into tiny pieces. Divide the tofu, vegetable, and fruit bits into the 2 bowls over the spinach and lettuce. Toss until well combined.

Sprinkle each bowl with 1 tablespoon (8 g) of dried cranberries or cherries and drizzle each bowl with the desired amount of dressing. Sprinkle ½ teaspoon hemp seeds over each bowl and serve.

Note

If making the elements in advance, toss the apple with lemon juice. There will be dressing leftover to use later on this salad or other salads. The dressing will keep for up to 3 weeks in an airtight container in the refrigerator.

Dustin's Favorite Summer Salad

This is a dream to take to a summer cookout. Its fresh ingredients are vibrant in color and flavor and very inviting when sitting on a table typically filled with chips, macaroni salad, and hot dogs. This was a staple of mine way before I even considered going vegan. To avoid the avocado getting brown, cut it fresh and add it to the salad once you get to the party.

1 pint (474 g) cherry tomatoes, halved

2 cups (328 g) fresh corn (or frozen, thawed to room temperature)

2 avocados, peeled and diced

¼ cup (10 g) fresh basil, roughly chopped

1 tablespoon (15 ml) olive oil

Juice of 1 lime

½ teaspoon sea salt, or more to taste

½ teaspoon black pepper, or more to taste

2 scallions, thinly sliced

Add the tomatoes, corn, avocado, basil, olive oil, lime juice, salt, and pepper to a large bowl. Mix until well combined. Sprinkle with additional salt and pepper, if desired. Top with scallions. Serve family style.

Note

When I have time, I like to sauté the corn in a dash of oil, salt, and pepper in a hot skillet just until lightly browned to get a rustic look. Then I let it cool and mix it with everything else. It's really a matter of preference. The fresh crunch of the corn uncooked is a delightful texture to pair with the creamy avocado, too!

Warm Rotini and Spinach Pesto Pasta Salad

YIELD: 4 SERVINGS

I love sneaking my greens in any way that I can, and what better way than tossing them with tasty carbs and this robust pesto sauce. This is a simple recipe to pull together on a Sunday afternoon when I'm working around the house or when guests pop over for an unannounced visit. I also love it as a meal-prep option. It's a nice comfort food to enjoy on hump day to get you through the midweek slump!

2 cups (195 g) rotini pasta or gluten-free pasta of choice

2 cups (60 g) baby spinach

1 cup (150 g) cherry tomatoes, halved

1 batch Presto Pesto (page 16)

Crushed red pepper (optional)

Cook the pasta according to package directions. Drain the pasta, and add the spinach and cherry tomatoes to the pot. Add the hot pasta back to the pot and top with pesto. Mix everything until well combined and the spinach has just slightly wilted. The spinach will still hold its shape some, but it will be softer and more malleable.

Serve warm sprinkled with crushed red pepper (if using).

Note

While this is meant to be served warm, you can absolutely portion it into meal-prep containers and eat it cold. You can also reheat it in the microwave or on the stovetop up to 3 days after making it. The green pesto will get darker in color when eaten as a leftover, but it's still edible and delicious.

Overstuffed Avocado Bowls

YIELD: 2 BOWLS

Avocados are so delicious with their buttery flavor, hint of nuttiness, and rich, creamy texture. They are the perfect addition to any meal, and in this case . . . the center of the meal! A good-for-you fat, avocados supply loads of vitamins (C, E, K, and B_6), beta-carotene, and omega-3 fatty acids! So, don't shy away from those calories when it comes to the beloved avocado. This is one of the cases where the calories are totally worth it.

3 cups (201 g) kale, stems removed, torn into bite-size pieces

2 teaspoons (10 ml) olive oil

1 teaspoon balsamic vinegar

1 large ripe avocado, halved, peeled with pit removed (see Note)

¼ cup (59 g) cooked quinoa

¼ cup (60 g) hummus

¼ cup (38 g) small-diced yellow bell pepper

¼ cup (35 g) small-diced cucumber

¼ cup (45 g) small-diced tomato

1 tablespoon (15 g) minced red onion

Juice of ½ lemon

¼ teaspoon sea salt

¼ teaspoon black pepper

Smoked paprika (optional)

Pepitas (optional)

Add the kale, oil, and balsamic to a bowl and massage the oil and vinegar into the kale with your hands for about 1 minute, until the liquid is evenly dispersed and the texture of the kale is softer. Divide the mixture into 2 smaller bowls and set an avocado half on top of each bed of kale.

In the same bowl the kale was massaged in, add the quinoa, hummus, bell pepper, cucumber, tomato, onion, lemon juice, salt, and pepper. Mix with a spoon until well combined.

Divide the mixture atop the avocados, filling the middle and overflowing into the bowl of kale. Sprinkle with smoked paprika and pepitas (if using).

Note

To half the avocado, slice through the avocado with a large knife lengthwise until you feel the knife hit the pit. Then rotate the avocado on the knife to make a cut around the pit. Twist the two halves apart. To remove the seed, aim the sharp edge of the knife blade at the pit and whack it hard enough so it sticks in the pit, then twist the knife to pull out the pit. To remove the skin, slip a spoon between the avocado and the skin. Carefully run the spoon along the edge, loosening the avocado from its skin.

Fiesta Quinoa Bowl
with Sweet Lime Vinaigrette

YIELD: 6 SERVINGS

This is not your average taco salad, but it's full of the robust flavors we know and love in a traditional taco bowl. This version is very grain-and-veggie forward with an abundance of greens. The irresistible sweet vinaigrette with spiced quinoa will satiate anyone's appetite. Pro tip on this simple and delicious vinaigrette is to double or triple the recipe to have some on hand in the refrigerator. It will last up to three weeks in an airtight container.

FOR THE SWEET LIME VINAIGRETTE

⅓ cup (80 ml) olive oil

Juice of 1½ limes

2 tablespoons (28 ml) agave

¼ teaspoon sea salt

FOR THE FIESTA QUINOA BOWL

3 cups (555 g) cooked quinoa

2 teaspoons (4 g) chili powder

2 cups (134 g) kale, stems removed and roughly chopped into small pieces

1 can (15 ounces [425 g]) black beans, drained and rinsed

1 red bell pepper, seeded and diced

1 cup (164 g) frozen or fresh corn, thawed if frozen

Sea salt

2 avocados, peeled and sliced

Almond cheese crumble

1 bunch scallions, thinly sliced (optional)

Pepitas (optional)

Chopped fresh cilantro (optional)

To make the sweet lime vinaigrette
Combine the oil, lime juice, agave, and salt in a bowl or container with an airtight lid or salad dressing shaker. Mix or shake with the sealed lid tightly on until well combined. Set aside.

To make the fiesta quinoa bowl
Combine the quinoa and chili powder in a bowl. Add the kale, black beans, bell pepper, and corn to the bowl, and mix until well combined. Add the lime vinaigrette to taste, and toss until well combined. Add salt to taste.

Serve in 1 big bowl family-style with avocados fanned out on top or portion into meal-prep containers for quick and easy meals throughout the week. If meal prepping, add the avocado fresh when consuming.

Garnish with almond cheese crumble, scallions, pepitas, and cilantro (if using).

Note

While this is meant to be served warm, you can absolutely portion it into meal-prep containers and eat it cold. You can also reheat it in the microwave or on the stovetop up to 3 days after making it. The green pesto will get darker in color when eaten as a leftover, but it's still edible and delicious.

Herbed Tofu Tomato Salad

YIELD: 4 SERVINGS

Pair the salty, herbed tofu cheese with ripe tomatoes, peppery baby arugula, and a squeeze of fresh lemon, and you have yourself a simple, seasonal salad that doubles as a great side dish.

1 package (12 ounces [340 g]) extra-firm tofu, rinsed and drained

½ cup (115 ml) water

1½ to 2 tablespoons (23 to 30 g) sea salt

2½ tablespoons (38 ml) coconut vinegar

2 tablespoons (28 ml) olive oil

1 teaspoon dried basil

1 teaspoon dried oregano

4 cups (720 g) chopped tomatoes

3 cups (60 g) packed baby arugula

1 tablespoon (15 ml) lemon juice

Pinch of black pepper

Pinch of coarse sea salt (optional)

Wrap the block of tofu tightly in a clean kitchen towel. Place it on a plate and stack some heavy (but stable) objects on it to press the moisture out. Let it press for 20 to 30 minutes.

In a resealable container or large zip-top plastic bag, whisk together the water, sea salt, coconut vinegar, olive oil, basil, and oregano.

Unwrap the pressed tofu, pat dry, cut it into ½-inch (1.3 cm) cubes, and place it in the marinade. Marinate it for 4 to 8 hours in the refrigerator, depending on how salty you would like it to be. Stir it around or flip the container over every couple of hours. Once the tofu is done marinating, drain it of the excess liquid and toss it together in a large bowl with the tomatoes and arugula.

Drizzle the lemon juice over the top of the salad and sprinkle on the pepper. Chill for 30 minutes and then sprinkle with sea salt, if using, and serve.

Note

If you don't have coconut vinegar, you should really get your hands on some! But if you can't find it, try replacing it with 1 tablespoon (15 ml) apple cider vinegar mixed with 1 tablespoon (16 g) white miso paste.

Roasted Pumpkin Quinoa Salad

Subtly sweet roasted pumpkin, fluffy red quinoa, and beautiful rainbow chard come together with a tangy dressing to create a wholesome autumnal salad that is delicious and satiating.

PLANT-BASED SIMPLE

2 pounds (910 g) pumpkin, peeled and cubed

1 tablespoon (15 ml) sunflower oil

⅛ teaspoon salt

1 cup (188 g) red quinoa

2 cups (475 ml) water

¼ cup (80 g) vegan honey (such as Bee Free Honee) or (60 ml) agave nectar

3 tablespoons (45 ml) apple cider vinegar

2 tablespoons (28 ml) olive oil

½ teaspoon crushed red pepper flakes

¼ teaspoon salt

½ pound (225 g) rainbow chard, chopped

Preheat the oven to 375°F (190°C, or gas mark 5) and line a baking sheet with parchment paper.

In a large bowl, toss the cubed pumpkin, sunflower oil, and salt together until evenly coated. Spread the pumpkin over the baking sheet and roast for 15 minutes. Flip the pumpkin pieces over, using a spoon, and roast for an additional 10 minutes.

While the pumpkin is roasting, place the quinoa and water in a large saucepan over medium-low heat and cover with the lid. Bring to a simmer and cook for 20 minutes or until the liquid is absorbed. Remove from the heat and fluff with a fork.

Whisk the vegan honey, apple cider vinegar, olive oil, red pepper flakes, and salt together until well combined. In a large bowl, toss the roasted pumpkin, quinoa, chard, and vinaigrette together. Serve immediately or chill in the refrigerator for 45 to 60 minutes before serving.

Asparagus Ribbon Salad

YIELD: 4 SERVINGS

Spring has so many gems to offer in terms of seasonal produce! Here we combine ribbons of asparagus with crisp, refreshing shaved fennel, creamy fava beans, and a sweet raisin vinaigrette to create a beautifully bright salad.

2 cups (475 ml) water

1 cup (150 g) fresh fava beans

6 ounces (170 g) asparagus

6 ounces (170 g) zucchini

6 ounces (170 g) fennel bulb

3 ounces (85 g) sunflower sprouts

⅓ cup (50 g) raisins, soaked in hot water to cover

3 tablespoons (45 ml) balsamic vinegar

1 tablespoon (15 ml) olive oil

⅛ teaspoon salt

⅛ teaspoon black pepper

1 cup (150 g) halved red grapes

¼ cup (36 g) roasted sunflower seeds

In a small pot, bring the water to a boil. Add the fava beans and cook for 4 minutes. Drain the beans and submerge them into a bowl of ice water for 2 minutes. Drain again, pop them out of their skins, and place in a small bowl.

Using a potato peeler, mandolin, or very sharp knife, cut the asparagus, zucchini, and fennel bulb into thin ribbons. Place them in a large bowl and add the sunflower sprouts.

Drain the raisins, reserving ¼ cup (60 ml) of the soaking water. Place the raisins, raisin soaking water, balsamic vinegar, olive oil, salt, and pepper in a blender and puree until smooth.

Toss the vinaigrette with the asparagus, zucchini, fennel, and sprouts. Top with the red grapes and sunflower seeds and serve.

Summery Stone Fruit Salad

YIELD: 4 SERVINGS

This fruity salad is simple but exquisite—so many beautiful slices of peaches, plums, nectarines, and cherries, speckled with bright green from the spinach and tingling mint. Up your fruit salad game at the next summer gathering with this stunner!

FOR THE STONE FRUIT SALAD

1 pound (455 g) white peaches, pitted and sliced

¾ pound (340 g) plums, pitted and sliced

6 ounces (170 g) nectarines, pitted and sliced

6 ounces (170 g) sweet dark cherries, pitted and halved

2 cups (60 g) packed ribbon-cut spinach

2 tablespoons (12 g) minced fresh mint

FOR THE MINT SIMPLE SYRUP

¼ cup (24 g) fresh mint leaves

2 tablespoons (28 ml) agave nectar

2 tablespoons (28 ml) lemon juice

Pinch of salt

To make the stone fruit salad
Toss the peaches, plums, nectarines, cherries, spinach, and mint together in a large bowl. Place them in the refrigerator to chill.

To make the mint simple syrup
Place the mint leaves in a glass measuring cup along with the agave nectar and muddle until the leaves have broken down. Whisk the lemon juice and salt into the mixture and strain it through a fine-mesh sieve over the fruit salad. Toss to coat everything evenly and serve.

Mighty Mango Pineapple Salad

YIELD: 4 SERVINGS

If you have ever sat at your desk at lunchtime, needing to be swept away to the tropical island of your (day) dreams, this salad would be the one to do it. A dish filled with juicy tropical fruits and coconutty cashews is certainly a memorable one.

FOR THE SALAD

2 cups (310 g) peeled and chopped pineapple

1 cup (175 g) peeled, seeded, and chopped mango

1 cup (175 g) peeled, seeded, and chopped papaya

1 cup (150 g) peeled and diced very ripe plantain

1 tablespoon (1 g) minced fresh cilantro

FOR THE CASHEWS

½ cup (70 g) raw cashews

1 tablespoon (15 ml) agave nectar

2 tablespoons (10 g) unsweetened shredded coconut

Pinch of salt

To make the salad

In a large bowl, toss the pineapple, mango, papaya, plantain, and cilantro until combined. Place in the refrigerator to chill while you prep the cashews.

To make the cashews

Preheat the oven to 300°F (150°C, or gas mark 2) and line a small baking sheet with parchment paper.

In a small bowl, toss the cashews and agave together until evenly coated. Add the coconut and salt to the bowl and stir gently. Spread the cashews out over the small baking sheet.

Bake for 5 minutes, stir them around to flip, and bake for another 5 minutes. Let cool for a few minutes. Top the fruit salad with the cashews and serve.

Grilled Romaine Chop Salad

YIELD: 2 SERVINGS

If you have never tried grilling greens before, you are missing out on one of my favorite ways to prepare them. This technique works really well with water-heavy greens like romaine, green leaf, and iceberg lettuces. Add smoky grilled eggplant and fresh veggies to the mix and you get a flavor explosion.

FOR THE SALAD

½ pound (225 g) eggplant, peeled and cut into ½-inch (1.3 cm)-thick rounds

2 teaspoons salt

2 tablespoons (28 ml) olive oil

1 tablespoon (15 ml) liquid aminos

1 teaspoon gluten-free liquid smoke

1 head romaine lettuce (1 pound [455 g]), quartered lengthwise

¼ pound (115 g) cremini mushrooms, stems removed

1 ear of corn, husk removed

1 cup (150 g) grape or cherry tomatoes, cut in half

1 cup (134 g) partially peeled and chopped cucumber

FOR THE DRESSING

2 tablespoons (28 ml) lemon juice

2 tablespoons (28 ml) olive oil

1½ teaspoons nutritional yeast

½ teaspoon Dijon mustard

¼ teaspoon agave nectar

⅛ teaspoon garlic powder

⅛ teaspoon salt

Pinch of black pepper

To make the salad

Lay the eggplant out on a plate and sprinkle each side with a light dusting of salt to release some of its juices. After 20 minutes, brush off as much salt as you can, pat the eggplant dry, and put the eggplant slices in a large zip-top plastic bag along with the olive oil, liquid aminos, and liquid smoke. Seal the bag, shake it up, and put it in the refrigerator to marinate for 30 minutes.

Prepare a medium-hot fire in a grill (350°F, or 180°C) and oil the grill grates.

Take the eggplant out of the marinade and set the marinade aside. Place the eggplant on the grill along with the romaine, mushrooms, and corn and cook for 3 to 5 minutes or until there are bold grill marks. Flip everything over and grill for an additional 3 to 5 minutes. Brush some of the leftover marinade over the eggplant for the last half of the grilling time.

Chop the romaine and eggplant into bite-size pieces. Cut the corn kernels off the cob. Divide the romaine between 2 bowls and top each bowl with eggplant, corn, mushrooms, tomatoes, and cucumber.

To make the dressing

Whisk all the ingredients together until smooth. Drizzle over the top of each salad and serve.

Autumn Salad with Citrus Vinaigrette

YIELD: 4 SERVINGS

Combining fruits with greens is a great way to liven up any salad, but adding farro for a savory, nutty flavor as well as maple-glazed pecans will give this beautiful dish priority on any holiday table.

SALADS

FOR THE GLAZED PECANS

½ cup (55 g) pecans

1 tablespoon (15 ml) water

1 tablespoon (15 ml) maple syrup

½ teaspoon ground cinnamon

½ teaspoon vanilla extract

Pinch of salt

FOR THE SALAD

½ cup (104 g) farro

1 cup (235 ml) water

5 ounces (140 g) mesclun greens

1 apple of your choice, cored and thinly sliced

1 Bosc pear, cored and thinly sliced

¼ cup (30 g) unsweetened dried cranberries

FOR THE VINAIGRETTE

¼ cup (60 ml) orange juice

3 tablespoons (45 ml) olive oil

1 tablespoon (15 ml) apple cider vinegar

1 tablespoon (15 ml) agave nectar

½ teaspoon grated orange zest

⅛ teaspoon ground ginger

Pinch of ground cinnamon

Pinch of salt

To make the glazed pecans
Place all the ingredients in a small saucepan over medium heat. Bring to a simmer and cook, stirring frequently, until most of the liquid has evaporated and the pecans are coated with the maple mixture. Transfer the pecans to a piece of parchment paper set on a cooling rack.

To make the salad
In a small pot over medium heat, bring the farro and water to a boil. Adjust the heat to medium-low, partially cover the pot with a lid, and cook for 20 to 25 minutes until the water is absorbed and the grains are cooked.

In a large serving bowl, toss the farro and mesclun mix. Arrange the apple and pear slices on top of the salad in a circular fashion and then top with the dried cranberries and glazed pecans.

To make the vinaigrette
Whisk together all the ingredients until emulsified. Serve the vinaigrette on the side.

Corn Salad with Basil Pesto Aioli

YIELD: 4 SERVINGS

This super-tasty side comes together in minutes! Summer corn plus basil pesto aioli is a dreamy combination, not to mention a great way to use up the basil that is oh-so-plentiful in the summer months.

FOR THE BASIL PESTO AIOLI

2 cups (60 g) packed baby spinach

1 cup (40 g) fresh basil leaves

2 tablespoons (28 ml) lemon juice

1 tablespoon (4 g) nutritional yeast

1 clove garlic, peeled

1 tablespoon (15 ml) olive oil

1 tablespoon (15 ml) water

½ teaspoon sea salt

¼ teaspoon black pepper

½ cup (112 g) vegan mayonnaise (soy-free, if necessary)

FOR THE SALAD

5 cups (820 g) cooked sweet yellow corn kernels

1 cup (30 g) packed ribbon-cut spinach

⅓ cup (55 g) sliced red onion

Salt and black pepper, to taste

To make the basil pesto aioli

Place the spinach, basil, lemon juice, nutritional yeast, garlic, olive oil, water, salt, and pepper in a food processor and puree until it becomes a paste. Scrape down the sides as necessary. Add the mayo to the processor and pulse until evenly combined.

To make the salad

Toss the corn, spinach, onion, and basil pesto aioli together in a medium bowl. Season with salt and pepper to taste and chill for 15 to 20 minutes before serving.

Tex-Mex Potato Salad

YIELD: 4 TO 6 SERVINGS

Cravable, creamy potato salad is spiced up with a pinch of cayenne and studded with black beans, corn, bell pepper, and more in this recipe.

¾ pound (340 g) multicolor fingerling potatoes, chopped

¼ cup (40 g) diced red onion

1 stalk celery, diced

½ cup (120 g) cooked black beans

½ cup (82 g) cooked sweet yellow corn kernels

½ cup (75 g) diced red bell pepper

½ cup (112 g) vegan mayonnaise

1 tablespoon (15 ml) apple cider vinegar

¼ teaspoon salt

Pinch of cayenne pepper

Place the potatoes in a large pot and cover them with water. Bring to a boil over medium-high heat and then adjust the heat to medium and cook for 20 minutes or until fork-tender. Drain the potatoes and transfer them to a bowl.

Add the red onion, celery, black beans, corn, bell pepper, mayo, apple cider vinegar, salt, and cayenne to the bowl and stir until combined. Stir together firmly to smash some of the potatoes slightly for a creamier potato salad.

Refrigerate the potato salad for 1 to 2 hours and serve chilled.

Deli-Style Chickpea Salad

YIELD: 10 SERVINGS

I believe the world cannot ever have enough recipes for a good chickpea salad. This one is mine, and I think it is quite divine. The creamy dressing has a sweet and tangy bite, which is mellowed out by the crunchy almonds and juicy grapes. This dish is equally amazing served on sliced bread or atop a bed of greens.

3½ cups (800 g) cooked chickpeas (if canned, drained and rinsed)

1 tablespoon (2.5 g) rubbed sage

1½ teaspoons chicken-flavored vegetable seasoning powder, such as McKay's (optional)

¼ teaspoon salt

3 stalks celery, thinly sliced (about 1 cup [100 g])

2 tablespoons (30 ml) lemon juice

½ cup (120 ml) vegan mayonnaise

1 tablespoon (15 g) spicy brown mustard

1 tablespoon (15 ml) agave nectar

¼ teaspoon celery salt

½ cup (60 g) sliced, toasted almonds

1 cup (150 g) quartered seedless grapes, any variety

In a food processor, combine the chickpeas, sage, veggie seasoning, and salt. Pulse briefly just until crumbly. Big pieces are totally fine, as are small . . . the size of the chickpea chunks will determine the texture of the salad. For a smoother salad, pulse the chickpeas longer.

Transfer to a bowl and stir in the celery, lemon juice, mayonnaise, brown mustard, agave, and celery salt until the salad is uniform in texture and color. Fold in the almonds and quartered grapes.

Serve on gluten-free bread or atop a bed of greens and devour!

Note

To easily toast sliced almonds, preheat the oven to 400°F (200°C, or gas mark 6), spread the nuts in a single layer on a baking sheet, and bake for 5 minutes or until fragrant.

Quinoa Tabbouleh

Instead of the traditional tabbouleh made with bulgur wheat, quinoa is used in this salad to make a gluten-free equivalent of the popular Lebanese dish.

1 cup (175 g) quinoa, rinsed and drained

2 cups (470 ml) water

¼ cup (60 ml) high-quality extra-virgin olive oil

1½ teaspoons sea salt

2 cups (120 g) finely minced fresh parsley

½ cup (30 g) finely minced fresh mint

3 medium-size tomatoes, seeded and diced

Zest and juice of 1 large lemon

½ teaspoon black pepper

3 scallions, finely chopped

Combine the quinoa and water in a 2-quart (2 L) saucepan. Bring the water to a boil over high heat. Immediately reduce the heat to a simmer, stir gently, and cover. Let simmer for about 15 minutes or until all the water has been absorbed. Chill the quinoa in the fridge until cold, about 1 hour.

Stir in the olive oil and salt and then gently fold in the parsley, mint, tomatoes, lemon juice and zest, pepper, and scallions until well combined. Let rest for at least 1 hour in the fridge until well chilled. Serve cold.

Note

Fresh mint and parsley are essential when making tabbouleh. The intense flavors of these herbs just don't come through well in dried varieties, and the fresh herbs add a nice texture and color to the salad.

Creamy Potato Salad

YIELD: 10 SERVINGS

This recipe for potato salad emulates the same recipe that my mother still makes to this day. Mine has a few extra add-ins and no animal products, but the flavor and texture are exactly as I remember as a child.

5 pounds (2.3 kg) Yukon gold potatoes, cut into 1-inch (2.5 cm) cubes

½ cup (120 ml) apple cider vinegar

5 tablespoons (70 ml) yellow mustard

2 cups (450 g) vegan mayonnaise

½ teaspoon sea salt

1 teaspoon celery salt

½ cup (75 g) minced red bell pepper

6 stalks celery, chopped to equal about 1 cup (150 g)

1 tablespoon (15 g) sweet relish

Paprika, to taste

Black pepper, to taste

Fill a large pot of water about halfway full with water, add 1 to 2 teaspoons sea salt, and bring to a rolling boil. Carefully add the potatoes and return the water to a rolling boil. Begin timing your potatoes when the water has returned to a full boil. Cook for about 7 minutes or just until they can be pierced with a fork but do not fall apart. These potatoes should not be cooked to the same consistency as you would cook mashed potatoes; you want them slightly less done than that.

Transfer the potatoes to a colander and drain well. While still in the colander, douse with vinegar, being sure to evenly cover. Place a plate under the colander and one on top to cover and place in the refrigerator until well chilled, about 2 hours.

Transfer the potatoes to a large mixing bowl and stir in the mustard, vegan mayonnaise, ½ teaspoon sea salt, celery salt, red bell pepper, celery, and relish. Stir well. If the potatoes seem to have held their shape too much, smash a few gently with a fork and then stir to once again incorporate the dressing.

Top with a good amount of paprika and pepper. Serve very cold.

Note

The cooking time on the potatoes is imperative to making the perfect potato salad. They should be easy to pierce with a fork but not *so* fork-tender that they fall apart when stirred. A nice middle ground should be met so that just a few potatoes break apart, creating a good base for the rest of the potatoes to swim in.

Spicy Edamame Coleslaw

YIELD: 8 SERVINGS

This coleslaw is slightly different than the typical American-style coleslaw because it features Asian-inspired flavors and coconut cream as the dressing base rather than mayo. It gets a little bit of a kick from the addition of sriracha and just may become your new favorite coleslaw.

FOR THE SLAW

1 small head napa cabbage

2 cups (260 g) frozen edamame

FOR THE DRESSING

1 ripe avocado, pitted and peeled

1 teaspoon freshly grated ginger

2 tablespoons (30 ml) mirin

3 tablespoons (45 ml) white miso

2 tablespoons (30 ml) rice vinegar

1 teaspoon wasabi powder, or to taste

4 heaping tablespoons (60 ml) full-fat coconut cream (the thickest part from a can of chilled, unstirred coconut milk)

¼ cup (60 ml) water

2 tablespoons (30 ml) agave nectar or (25 g) sugar

1 tablespoon (15 ml) spicy chili garlic sauce (such as sriracha), or to taste

To make the slaw

Shred the cabbage and place in a large bowl.

Boil the edamame just until tender, about 5 minutes. Once done, rinse under cold water until no longer hot and drain well. Toss with the shredded cabbage and mix until the edamame is evenly distributed throughout.

To make the dressing

In a bowl, use a fork to mash the avocado and then vigorously mix in the remaining ingredients until smooth. If needed, process in a blender or food processor; there should be no lumps in the dressing.

Toss the cabbage and edamame with the dressing until evenly coated. Serve immediately.

Notes

You can leave the chili garlic sauce out of the initial mixing of the dressing and just drizzle on top to taste for each individual serving. This works especially well if you're sharing with little kiddos or folks who aren't down with hot and spicy.

The best way to get the thick cream from a can of coconut cream is to chill the entire can in your fridge overnight. All the thick cream will rise and sit on top of the coconut water. Then you can simply scoop it out without worrying about separating. I have found that Whole Foods' brand of full-fat coconut milk works exceptionally well with this method.

Late Summer Salad
with Creamy Dill Dressing

YIELD: 8 SERVINGS

This is a creamy twist on a summer salad I have been making since I was a child. I always got such joy from eating this salad in late July or August when our garden was abundant with vine-ripened tomatoes, fresh dill, and crisp cucumbers. Today, I still recommend sourcing ingredients from a local garden and eating in the shade of a tree while sprawled out on a blanket in the grass.

4 or 5 medium-size tomatoes

1 or 2 medium-size cucumbers, peeled

3 tablespoons (45 ml) apple cider vinegar

1 package (15 ounces [420 g]) silken tofu

1 or 2 cloves garlic (2 makes it extra tangy)

1 teaspoon salt, or to taste

5 tablespoons (20 g) chopped fresh dill, divided, plus several sprigs for garnish

Chop the tomatoes and cucumbers into bite-size pieces. Toss with the apple cider vinegar and let marinate for at least 30 minutes in the fridge.

In a food processor, combine the silken tofu, garlic, salt, and 2 tablespoons (8 g) of the fresh dill. Puree until very smooth.

Remove the cucumbers and tomatoes from the refrigerator, drain well, and toss with enough dressing to thoroughly coat. Depending on the size of your veggies, you may be left with a little extra dressing.

Stir in the remaining 3 tablespoons (12 g) fresh dill. Chill in the refrigerator until cold, about 1 hour, although this dish is wonderful if you let the flavors meld for a few hours before serving. Garnish with a fresh sprig of dill and serve cold.

Note

The original version of this salad can be easily made by omitting the garlic and tofu. Instead of draining the vinegar, let it remain as the base for the dressing. It is a bit lighter and a perfect snack for a hot summertime afternoon.

Eggplant and Cucumber Salad

YIELD: 4 SERVINGS

Korean inspiration shines through in this salad with the combination of crispy cold cucumbers and warm tender eggplant. I took a cue from cucumber banchan, a favorite salad that I used to enjoy quite often during my college years, to create this unique dish.

FOR THE EGGPLANT MIX

3 Japanese eggplants (about 1.3 pounds [600 g]), peeled, halved, and cut into large bite-size pieces

¼ cup (25 g) chopped scallion

1 tablespoon (10 g) minced garlic

1 tablespoon (4 g) minced fresh oregano

2 tablespoons (30 ml) olive oil

¼ cup (60 ml) water

1 teaspoon salt

1 tablespoon (15 g) horseradish (freshly grated or jarred, not powdered)

FOR THE CUCUMBER MIX

1 large English (or thin-skinned) cucumber, diced

2 tablespoons (8 g) chopped fresh oregano

Zest and juice of 1 lemon

1 teaspoon sea salt

2 tablespoons (30 ml) olive oil

1 tablespoon (15 ml) agave nectar

To prepare the eggplant mix

Combine the eggplant, scallion, garlic, oregano, and olive oil in a medium-size saucepan and cook over medium-high heat until soft, about 8 minutes.

Add the water, salt, and horseradish and cover with a tight-fitting lid. Reduce the heat to medium-low and cook about 10 minutes longer, stirring occasionally so that the eggplant doesn't stick to the pan. Remove from the heat and let cool to room temperature.

To prepare the cucumber mix

In a large bowl, combine the diced cucumber, oregano, lemon juice and zest, salt, olive oil, and agave. Cover and let rest in the refrigerator for about 20 minutes, allowing the eggplant to come to room temperature as you wait.

Drain the excess liquid from the cucumber mix and toss with the eggplant. Serve at room temperature or chill before serving.

Orange, Artichoke, Arugula, and Fennel Salad

YIELD: 4 SERVINGS

The various flavors and textures of this salad work so perfectly together that only a touch of dressing is needed to make a fantastic dish. I've always thought arugula to have an almost walnut-like flavor, which adds a nice earthy balance to the bright notes of the fennel and orange.

2 tablespoons (30 ml) freshly squeezed lemon juice

1 tablespoon (15 ml) extra-virgin olive oil

1 tablespoon (15 ml) agave nectar

2 tablespoons (30 ml) freshly squeezed orange juice

1 teaspoon poppy seeds, plus a pinch for garnish

2 packed cups (58 g) baby arugula leaves

½ cup (100 g) thinly shaved fennel bulb, tough core removed (use a mandolin or a vegetable peeler)

8 small canned artichoke hearts, halved

2 medium-size seedless oranges, supremed (see Note)

In a medium-size bowl, whisk together the lemon juice, olive oil, agave, orange juice, and poppy seeds to make a thin dressing. Toss with the baby arugula leaves to evenly and lightly coat.

Gently stir in the shaved fennel, artichoke hearts, and oranges. Garnish with a pinch of poppy seeds and serve immediately.

Note

To supreme an orange, cut off the top and bottom of the orange so that the fruit sits flat on your cutting board and the interior of the orange is visible. Carefully cut the remaining peel off, following the curve of the fruit, until no more pith remains on the outside of the flesh. Over a bowl to catch the juice, cut along the membrane of each section with your knife from top to bottom and slice through to reveal each orange wedge. After cutting through the center of the membrane, the segments can easily be removed.

SALADS

Drenched Pad Thai Salad

YIELD: 6 SERVINGS

Even though this salad has zucchini "noodles," I find it hearty enough to serve as a meal because it contains grilled pineapple and tofu.

1 package (16 ounces [455 g]) extra-firm tofu, well drained and pressed

FOR THE TOFU MARINADE

¾ cup (175 ml) pineapple juice

3 scallions, thinly sliced

2 cloves garlic, minced

3 tablespoons (45 ml) wheat-free tamari or soy sauce

1 teaspoon Chinese five-spice powder

1 teaspoon peanut oil or olive oil

1 can (15 ounces [420 g]) pineapple slices in pineapple juice

2 or 3 zucchini

FOR THE SALAD DRESSING

¾ cup (180 ml) liquid from tofu marinade

2 tablespoons (30 ml) lime juice

4 heaping tablespoons (64 g) smooth peanut butter

Wheat-free tamari or soy sauce, to taste

FOR THE SALAD

1 mango cut into bite-size pieces

½ cup (110 g) roasted peanuts, crushed

Chopped fresh cilantro (optional)

Favorite hot sauce (optional)

Slice the pressed tofu block in half, making 2 rectangles about ½ inch (1.3 cm) thick, and then cut into bite-size triangles. Arrange the tofu in a single layer in a medium-size baking dish.

To make the tofu marinade

Whisk all the tofu marinade ingredients together and then pour the marinade over the tofu. Let marinate for at least 2 hours, flipping the tofu halfway through. Remove the tofu from the dish, reserving the leftover marinade.

Place the tofu on an electric indoor grill (or mesh grill pan placed on an outdoor grill) and cook until golden brown on both sides, 10 to 15 minutes. Grill the pineapple rings.

To make your zucchini noodles, remove the ends from the zucchini and peel if desired. Using a vegetable spiralizer or vegetable peeler, cut the zucchini into long noodlelike strips and place in a large bowl.

To make the salad dressing

Whisk together all the dressing ingredients until smooth. The dressing will be quite soupy. Add a touch more tamari to taste, if desired. Pour the dressing over the zucchini noodles and mix together until well coated, allowing the excess to remain at the bottom of the bowl.

To assemble the salad

Divide the drenched zucchini noodles among separate bowls, also transferring some dressing to each bowl. Top with the grilled tofu, mango, grilled pineapples, crushed peanuts, cilantro, and hot sauce. Serve.

Asparagus Orzo Salad

YIELD: 5 SERVINGS

This asparagus orzo salad screams spring! Instead of blanching the asparagus, I sauté it to add another layer of flavor to the fresh herbs and bright lemon juice. If you're looking for an easy-to-make, mood-lifting dish, this one is perfect.

2 cups (320 g) orzo, gluten-free if desired

2 teaspoons sunflower oil

8 ounces (225 g) asparagus, woody ends removed, chopped

2 cups (310 g) frozen peas, thawed

¾ cup (105 g) pine nuts or sunflower seeds

4 cups (120 g) firmly packed baby arugula

½ cup (58 g) sliced radishes

¼ cup (25 g) diced scallion

¼ to ⅓ cup (60 to 80 ml) lemon juice

2 tablespoons (5 g) chopped dill

2 tablespoons (8 g) chopped parsley

1 tablespoon (15 ml) olive oil (optional)

½ teaspoon salt

¼ teaspoon black pepper

Prepare the orzo according to the package instructions; when just past al dente, drain and rinse with cold water. Set aside to fully cool. While the orzo is cooking, heat the sunflower oil in a large skillet over medium heat. Add the asparagus and cook until it begins to brown, 5 to 7 minutes.

Add the peas and the pine nuts to the pan and cook, stirring often, until the nuts are toasted and golden in color, 1 to 2 minutes. Transfer the asparagus mixture to a large bowl and let cool to room temperature. Add the cooled orzo and the arugula, radishes, scallion, lemon juice, dill, parsley, and olive oil, if using, to the bowl. Season with the salt and pepper and chill for 10 minutes before serving. Salad can be stored in the refrigerator for up to 7 days.

Tropical Cucumber Chili Salad

YIELD: 4 SERVINGS

In Southern California, you'd be hard-pressed to miss the fruit carts on so many street corners. On a hot summer day, they're heaven sent, and topping their fruit cups with Tajín, a Mexican spice mix, makes them even better. This salad was inspired by those flavors.

1½ pounds (680 g) cucumbers, spiralized

1½ cups (233 g) diced pineapple

1 cup (175 g) diced mango

½ cup (50 g) halved and thinly sliced red onion

½ cup (8 g) loosely packed chopped cilantro

2 tablespoons (30 ml) lime juice

1 cup (137 g) roasted cashews

1 tablespoon (8 g) chili powder

½ teaspoon salt

Pinch cayenne pepper

In a large bowl, combine spiralized cucumber, pineapple, mango, onion, cilantro, and lime juice. Divide between 4 bowls or storage containers and top with roasted cashews. In a small bowl or ramekin, combine the chili powder, salt, and cayenne. Sprinkle salad with chili seasoning just before serving. Unseasoned salad can be stored in the refrigerator for up to 7 days.

Note

If you do not have a spiralizer, you can make cucumber noodles with a julienne peeler or a standard vegetable peeler.

CHAPTER FIVE
Main Dishes

Stovetop Mushroom Tetrazzini

YIELD: 8 SERVINGS

My mother used to make a really tasty chicken tetrazzini bake when I was a kid, and I have been wanting to make one for some time. I love the robust flavors paired with the joy and comfort pasta inevitably brings to the table. And this stovetop version comes together so quickly. With everything being cooked in one pot, you don't even have to drain the pasta. And hey, a little fun fact, tetrazzini is actually named after the Italian opera star Luisa Tetrazzini. I thank Lady Tetrazzini for this abundant dish of Italian goodness!

¼ cup (55 g) vegan butter

1 onion, diced

16 ounces (454 g) sliced baby bella or cremini mushrooms

6 cloves garlic

2 tablespoons (28 ml) white wine vinegar

4 cups (940 ml) vegetable broth

1 pound (454 g) spaghetti

1½ cups (225 g) frozen peas

½ cup (40 g) nutritional yeast

¼ cup (30 g) bread-crumbs or gluten-free breadcrumbs

1½ teaspoons sea salt

½ teaspoon black pepper

1 tablespoon (15 g) Italian seasoning

¼ cup (15 g) chopped fresh parsley

Crushed red pepper (optional)

Melt the butter in a stockpot over medium heat. Add the onion and mushrooms. Sauté for 4 to 6 minutes, until the mushrooms have reduced in size. Add the garlic and sauté for 1 minute, until fragrant. Add the white wine vinegar and sauté for 2 to 4 minutes, until the vinegar evaporates.

Add the vegetable broth and bring to a boil. Add the spaghetti, breaking it if need be so it fits in the pan submerged by the broth. Continue to boil and cook the pasta according to the package directions, stirring occasionally to keep the noodles from sticking and moving them around to cook evenly. Add the peas to the pot in the final 2 minutes of cooking. Do not drain the pasta.

When the pasta is cooked to your liking (al dente suggested), add the nutritional yeast, breadcrumbs, salt, pepper, Italian seasoning, and parsley. Toss until everything is well combined and the pasta is evenly coated. Divide into serving bowls and garnish with crushed red pepper (if using).

Note

Use 1 pound (454 g) of your favorite type of pasta in place of the spaghetti if you wish! Using a smaller pasta makes it easier to mix up the ingredients. Traditionally tetrazzini is made with a long pasta, and I also prefer spaghetti, but I encourage you to pick your favorite or use whatever type you have on hand.

Mediterranean Spaghetti Squash

YIELD: 4 SERVINGS

When I first started learning to cook for myself, I remember being so amazed at how you could use spaghetti squash as a replacement for pasta. Combine the ease of its preparation with the Mediterranean flavors of olives, eggplant, and chickpeas for this great weeknight meal.

3 pounds (1.4 kg) spaghetti squash

1 tablespoon (15 ml) olive oil

2 cloves garlic, minced

10 ounces (280 g) eggplant, chopped

1 can (15 ounces [425 g]) chickpeas, rinsed and drained

½ cup (28 g) julienne-cut dry-pack sun-dried tomatoes

½ cup (70 g) Kalamata olives, sliced

2 tablespoons (18 g) capers with brine

1 teaspoon dried oregano

2 cups (60 g) packed baby spinach

1 teaspoon salt

Pinch of crushed red pepper flakes

Preheat the oven to 350°F (180°C, or gas mark 4) and pour ¼ inch (6 mm) water into the bottom of a large baking dish.

Cut the spaghetti squash in half lengthwise and poke a few holes in the rind with a fork. Lay the squash cut side down in the baking dish and bake for 40 to 45 minutes until fork-tender. Let cool for 10 minutes.

Heat the olive oil in a large sauté pan, with high walls, over medium heat. Sauté the garlic in the oil for 1 minute and then add the eggplant. Brown the eggplant for 2 minutes and then flip it over and brown for an additional 2 minutes.

Scrape the spaghetti squash strands into the pan and add the chickpeas, sun-dried tomatoes, olives, capers, and oregano. Cook for 5 minutes over medium-low heat and then fold in the spinach, salt, and red pepper flakes. Sauté just until the spinach has wilted. Serve hot.

Instant Pot Spaghetti Squash with Pistachio Sage Sauce

YIELD: 4 SERVINGS

Even though I love spaghetti squash, it usually takes some time to get the dang thing roasted or steamed. Not with this multicooker method! Even with the time it takes to get to pressure, the process is only a fraction of what it would take in the oven—and with a large squash, too!

1 (4 pounds [1815 g]) spaghetti squash

1 cup (123 g) shelled raw pistachios plus ¼ cup (35 g) chopped roasted pistachios

2 cups (475 ml) vegetable broth

1 cup (89 g) chopped leeks

1½ teaspoons ground sage

1 teaspoon dried thyme

½ teaspoon salt

¼ teaspoon black pepper

1 teaspoon red wine vinegar

Cut the spaghetti squash into 4 round slices, scoop out the seeds, and arrange on a rack in your Instant Pot or multicooker. Add 1 cup (235 ml) water, then close the lid and bring to high pressure. Once the pot reaches high pressure, cook for 7 minutes, then turn off the heat and let sit for 3 minutes before quick-releasing the pressure. Remove the lid and allow the squash to cool for 10 minutes before handling.

While the squash is cooking, put the raw pistachios in a small pot and cover them with water. Bring to a boil, then adjust the heat to medium-low and simmer, covered, for 5 minutes. Drain and rinse the pistachios and transfer them to a blender, adding the vegetable broth, leeks, sage, thyme, salt, and pepper. Puree until smooth, then let sit for 5 minutes before pureeing again.

Transfer the sauce to a skillet, add the vinegar, and simmer over medium-low heat, stirring occasionally, for 5 minutes. Pull the squash from the skin with a fork and divide it between 4 bowls or storage containers, then top with the sauce and the roasted pistachios. Serve warm or store in the refrigerator for up to 7 days or in the freezer for up to 3 months.

Baked Not So Stir-Fry in a Flash

YIELD: 6 SERVINGS

I always get impatient when frying tofu, but I found I could skip all that by adding all my favorite stir-fry goodies to a sheet pan, baking it in the oven, and setting my table for dinner while it cooks! The muss and fuss of standing over the stove monitoring my tofu is gone from the equation in this version bursting with fresh vegetables, Chinese spice, and succulent tofu.

½ red onion, cut into chunks

1 red bell pepper, roughly chopped

½ head broccoli, stems removed, cut into bite-size florets

8 ounces (225 g) baby bella mushrooms, stemmed and sliced

1 package (14 ounces [396 g]) extra-firm tofu, cut into ½-inch (1 cm) cubes

2 tablespoons (30 ml) sesame oil

3 tablespoons (45 ml) soy sauce

1 teaspoon Chinese five-spice powder (optional)

½ teaspoon sea salt

½ teaspoon garlic powder

Rice, cauliflower rice, or quinoa

Preheat the oven to 425°F (220°C, or gas mark 7). Line a sheet pan with parchment paper.

In a large bowl, combine the onion, bell pepper, broccoli, mushrooms, and tofu. Drizzle with sesame oil and soy sauce, and gently toss until everything is coated. Add the Chinese five-spice powder (if using), salt, and garlic powder, and gently toss to coat.

Transfer to the prepared sheet pan and spread in 1 layer. Bake for 15 minutes, flip everything, and bake for 15 minutes, until the tofu has started to lightly crisp up and the broccoli has started to char.

Serve with rice, cauliflower rice, or quinoa for a complete dish.

Note

Traditionally used in Chinese cuisine, Chinese five-spice powder is a great spice to have on hand. I like to use it as a rub for tofu, seitan, and tempeh. I want to stress that if you don't have it and don't plan on buying it, that's okay! Simply omit it from this recipe and it will still be tasty.

Cashew-Crusted Tofu Stir-Fry

YIELD: 4 SERVINGS

Stir-fries and vegetable sautés were just about all I lived on when I first went vegan. Making them is such a simple way to get tons of nutrients and flavor, all in a weeknight mealtime slot.

FOR THE TOFU

1 package (12 ounces [340 g]) extra-firm tofu, drained

¼ cup (35 g) raw cashews

3 tablespoons (30 g) rice flour

½ teaspoon salt

¼ teaspoon ground ginger

¼ teaspoon garlic powder

1½ tablespoons (21 g) coconut oil

FOR THE STIR-FRY

1 tablespoon (14 g) coconut oil

1 tablespoon (8 g) grated fresh ginger

2 cloves garlic, minced

3 scallions, cut into 1-inch (2.5 cm) pieces

1 head baby bok choy, cut into 8 wedges

1 large carrot, sliced into coins

1 cup (71 g) chopped baby broccoli

1 cup (150 g) sliced orange bell pepper

1 cup (75 g) sugar snap peas

3 tablespoons (45 ml) sherry cooking wine

3 tablespoons (45 ml) liquid aminos or tamari

FOR SERVING

2 cups (370 g) cooked quinoa (optional)

To make the tofu

Wrap the tofu in a clean kitchen towel. Place it on a plate and stack some heavy (but stable) objects on it for 15 minutes to press the moisture out. In a food processor, pulse the cashews until they resemble coarse sand. Combine the cashews, rice flour, salt, ginger, and garlic powder in a shallow dish.

Slice the tofu into 12 rectangles and melt the coconut oil in a large skillet over medium heat. Firmly press the tofu into the cashew mixture, coating all sides, and gently place each slice in the hot pan. Cook for 3 to 5 minutes on each side until golden brown. Turn the stove off and keep the tofu warm in the skillet while you start the stir-fry.

To make the stir-fry

In a large skillet or wok, melt the coconut oil over medium-high heat. Add the ginger, garlic, and scallions and sauté for 1 minute or until fragrant. Place the bok choy, carrot, broccoli, bell pepper, and sugar snap peas in the skillet and sear for 3 minutes.

Stir the veggies around and sear for 3 more minutes. Deglaze the pan with the sherry and liquid aminos and stir-fry until the broccoli is tender but not soggy.

To serve

Divide the quinoa (if using) and stir-fried veggies among 4 bowls, top each one with 3 pieces of tofu, and serve.

Sesame Miso Stir-Fry

YIELD: 4 SERVINGS

If ever there is a day where you think to yourself, "You know, I haven't really had many vegetables," this dish will totally solve your problem! This beautifully green stir-fry has a variety of veggies and is lightly coated with a simple sesame miso sauce.

FOR THE RICE

2⅔ cups (630 ml) water

1⅓ cups (259 g) short-grain white rice

1 tablespoon (15 ml) toasted sesame oil, divided

FOR THE STIR-FRY

2 cups (230 g) halved and sliced yellow onion

8 ounces (225 g) baby broccoli or broccolini, cut in half widthwise

2 cups (180 g) chopped green cabbage

2 heads baby bok choy, each sliced into 6 pieces lengthwise

1 tablespoon (15 ml) tamari

1 tablespoon (15 ml) unseasoned rice vinegar

1 tablespoon (16 g) white miso paste

3 cloves garlic, minced

1 teaspoon agave nectar

1 cup (140 g) edamame

To make the rice in a multicooker

Place 1⅔ cups (395 ml) water and the rice into the multicooker pot. Bring to high pressure, cooking for 19 minutes, and let sit for 5 minutes, then quick-release the rest of the pressure.

To make the rice on the stovetop

In a pot, bring the water and rice to a boil over medium heat. Cover the pot and adjust the heat to medium-low. Simmer until the rice is tender and liquid is absorbed, about 20 minutes. Fluff with a fork and set aside.

To make the stir-fry

In a large skillet or wok, heat 2 teaspoons of the toasted sesame oil over high heat. Add the onions and cook for 2 minutes, stirring occasionally. Add the broccoli, cabbage, and bok choy to the skillet and cook until there is some browning and the veggies have softened a little, 3 to 5 minutes. Meanwhile, in a small bowl, whisk together the remaining sesame oil and the tamari, rice vinegar, miso paste, garlic, and agave nectar.

Adjust the heat to medium-low and add the sauce and the edamame to the skillet, stirring to coat; cook for 2 more minutes. Divide the rice between 4 bowls or storage containers. Top with the stir-fry and serve immediately, or store in the refrigerator for up to 7 days or in the freezer for up to 3 months.

Note

The sauce may seem nearly nonexistent at first, but once the sodium from the tamari hits the veggies, they will start to release water, increasing the volume of sauce. If you'd like more of it, just add 2 to 4 tablespoons (30 to 60 ml) water to the sauce before adding it to the skillet.

Toasty Pear, Walnut, and Arugula Flatbread

YIELD: 12 PIECES

Naan is a perfect option for a quick flatbread, but sometimes a vegan naan can be hard to find. A thin-crust pizza dough will work just fine or even a tortilla in a pinch (see Note). The subtle, juicy, fruit-forward sweetness of the pears with the creamy hummus and zippy dash of balsamic make this flatbread an impressive quick dinner to serve friends at wine-o-clock!

12 oz (340 g) store-bought vegan thin-crust pizza dough or pizza dough

2 tablespoons (30 ml) olive oil, divided

1 package (10 ounces [280 g]) store-bought hummus

1 cup (235 g) pear, cored and thinly sliced

½ cup (58 g) red onion, thinly sliced

½ cup (60 g) walnuts, chopped

½ cup (57 g) vegan mozzarella shreds

1 cup (20 g) baby arugula

2 pinches sea salt

2 tablespoons (28 ml) balsamic glaze

Preheat the oven to 425°F (220°C, or gas mark 7). Line a large sheet pan with parchment paper.

Roll or stretch the pizza dough to fit the sheet pan. Brush the dough with 1 tablespoon plus 2 teaspoons (25 ml) olive oil. Place the sheet pan in the oven and bake for 4 minutes.

Remove from the oven and spread the hummus in one layer over the dough. Add the pear slices, onion, and walnuts, and sprinkle with mozzarella until evenly covered. Return to the oven and bake for 12 to 14 minutes, until the cheese is melted and the edges of flatbread have browned.

While the flatbread is baking, add the arugula and remaining olive oil to a bowl with salt. Toss until arugula is evenly coated.

Remove the pizza from the oven. Top with the dressed arugula, and drizzle with balsamic glaze.

Note

If you are struggling to find vegan naan or pizza dough, use two burrito-size tortillas to make your flatbread. Since the tortillas are so thin, only brush each tortilla with 1 teaspoon of olive oil and prebake for just 3 minutes before adding toppings to avoid burning.

Bow-Tie Alfredo with Broccoli and Sun-Dried Tomatoes

YIELD: 10 TO 12 SERVINGS

When I think of Alfredo, I think of creamy decadence and this sauce offers up just that! I like bow-tie (farfalle) pasta because of its fun shape and it's easy to fork. If you prefer your Alfredo with fettuccine, I certainly won't stop you! Add vegan chicken atop this dish for a nostalgic twist.

FOR THE ALFREDO SAUCE

1½ cups (205 g) raw cashews, soaked overnight or boiled for 10 minutes and drained

2 cups (475 ml) water

1 teaspoon garlic powder

1 teaspoon onion powder

2 teaspoons (10 g) sea salt

Juice of ½ lemon

3 tablespoons (15 g) nutritional yeast

½ teaspoon dried rosemary

¾ teaspoon black pepper

FOR THE PASTA

1 pound (454 g) bow-tie pasta

1 head broccoli, cut into bite-size florets

1 cup (55 g) sun-dried tomatoes, roughly chopped

To make the Alfredo sauce

Combine the cashews, water, garlic powder, onion powder, salt, lemon juice, nutritional yeast, rosemary, and pepper in a blender. Blend for 1 to 2 minutes, until smooth and creamy.

To make the pasta

Cook the pasta according to package directions. During the last 2 minutes of cooking, add the broccoli and sun-dried tomatoes to the boiling water. Cook until the desired doneness of pasta is reached (al dente is recommended).

Drain the pasta and vegetables, and then return them to the pot they were cooked in. Add the sauce to the pasta and vegetables, and mix until everything is coated. Serve warm.

Note

The Alfredo sauce can be made ahead of time and kept in an airtight container in the refrigerator for up to 1 week. It's great to have on hand to mix with freshly cooked pasta for a quick dinner or lunch.

One-Pan Super Saucy Garlic Ziti

YIELD: 8 TO 10 SERVINGS

Pasta and sauce would be my meal of choice—all day, every day—if I had it my way! I love this simple quick roast of garlic to add a punch of garlicky goodness to this traditional saucy dish. The main issue I always have with ziti is that it isn't saucy enough because the pasta soaks up the sauce when it bakes. I took care of that here, upping the sauce game, so you get those robust sauce flavors and your carbs with every spoonful.

12 cloves garlic, halved

½ onion, roughly chopped

¼ cup (59 ml) olive oil

1 pound (454 g) ziti or penne pasta, cooked

2 cups (228 g) vegan mozzarella shreds, divided

½ teaspoon sea salt

¼ teaspoon crushed red pepper, plus more for sprinkling

¼ teaspoon black pepper

2 jars (24 ounces [682 ml]) marinara

Italian seasoning (optional)

Preheat the oven to 375°F (190°C, or gas mark 5).

Add the garlic, onions, and olive oil to a 9 × 13-inch (23 × 33 cm) baking dish. Bake for 16 minutes, until the garlic has started to brown slightly and the onions have slightly reduced in size.

Remove the baking dish from the oven. Add the cooked pasta, 1½ cups (171 g) mozzarella shreds, salt, crushed red pepper, pepper, and marinara to the baking dish. Mix everything until well combined. Top with the remaining mozzarella, Italian seasoning (if using), and more crushed red pepper if desired.

Bake for 30 minutes, until the cheese has melted and edges are bubbling.

Coco Loco Pad Thai

YIELD: 6 SERVINGS PAD THAI AND 2 CUPS (475 ML) SAUCE

Creamy, luscious, and decadent is what I think of when I think of coconut. Paired with the divine peanut, it's the sauce of all sauces. Drizzle it on veggies, toss baked tofu in it, or use it as a dip! You can always stay on the healthy side and use it with spiralized noodles. It really is a great sauce to have on hand to take your meal prep to the next level.

FOR THE COCO LOCO PEANUT SAUCE

¾ cup (175 ml) canned coconut milk

¼ cup (80 g) maple syrup

2 tablespoons (28 ml) soy sauce or gluten-free tamari

Juice of ½ lime

1 tablespoon (15 ml) seasoned rice vinegar

1 tablespoon (15 ml) toasted sesame oil

½ cup (130 g) creamy peanut butter

1 tablespoon (15 ml) chili garlic sauce

½ teaspoon ginger powder

½ teaspoon garlic powder

¼ teaspoon sea salt

FOR THE PAD THAI

1 box (14 ounces [396 g]) thin rice noodles

2 tablespoons (30 ml) toasted sesame oil, divided

1 red bell pepper, thinly sliced

1 cup (235 g) shredded or matchstick carrot

1 bunch scallions, cut into 2-inch (5 cm) strips

Canned or fresh bean sprouts, drained

Crushed peanuts (optional)

Lime wedges (optional)

Chopped fresh cilantro (optional)

To make the coco loco peanut sauce

Shake the can of coconut up to make sure the liquid and fat mix together well. Add the ¾ cup (175 ml) of coconut milk, maple syrup, soy sauce, lime juice, vinegar, oil, peanut butter, chili garlic sauce, ginger powder, garlic powder, and salt to a blender. Blend until smooth and creamy.

To make the pad thai

Cook the noodles according to package directions, drain, and toss with 1 tablespoon (15 ml) of sesame oil. In the same pot the noodles were cooked in, heat the remaining sesame oil. Add the bell pepper and carrot. Sauté for 2 to 4 minutes, until starting to soften. Add the scallions and cook for 1 minute, until soft. Add the pasta and peanut sauce, and toss until combined. Divide among 6 bowls and garnish with sprouts, crushed peanuts, and cilantro (if using). Serve warm.

Note

The sauce thickens on the pasta as it sets. If you serve as a leftover, drizzle 1 to 2 tablespoons (15 to 28 ml) of water over the pasta and mix in while reheating on the stovetop. Use more water as needed to loosen it back up until the pasta is heated through.

Fuss-Free French Bread Pizzas

Raise your hand if frozen French bread pizzas were your jam when you were a kid. I'm raising both of my hands because of these and pizza rolls. In this vegan version, I use the broiler so the insides of the bread stay fluffy and get warm while the outside gets crispy giving you the perfect bite with a flaky crust and pillowy bread on the inside. I stick with cheese, but add your favorite pizza toppings if you prefer a loaded French bread pizza.

1 French baguette, cut into a 6-inch (15 cm)-long piece, halved (see Note)

¼ cup (60 ml) marinara

¼ cup (59 g) vegan mozzarella shreds

1 teaspoon olive oil

Toppings of choice (optional)

¼ teaspoon Italian seasoning

Crushed red pepper (optional)

Preheat the oven to broil.

Place each side of the baguette with the cut side of the baguette facing up. Divide the marinara between each baguette half and spread generously over the tops. Divide the mozzarella between the baguettes and drizzle ½ teaspoon of olive oil over the mozzarella. Add toppings (if using). Sprinkle Italian seasoning over each half and add crushed red pepper (if using).

Broil for 3 minutes. Rotate the pan and broil for 3 more minutes, until the cheese has melted and the edges have just started to brown. Remove from the oven and let cool to the touch. Serve warm.

Remember, all broilers have different intensities. Keep an eye on the bread. If you find that after the first 3 minutes the cheese is melted and the edges have started to brown, there is no need to continue broiling.

Note

There's no such thing as a baguette that is only 6 inches (15 cm) long. I wanted to clarify before you spend hours at the supermarket losing your mind. Get a French baguette or Italian loaf of bread and slice off 6 inches. How do you determine what 6 inches is? Use a ruler.

Punk Cheddah Mac Bake

YIELD: 10 TO 12 SERVINGS MAC BAKE AND 4 CUPS (940 ML) SAUCE

This sauce is a very mild and smooth sauce that's simple to make because it uses canned pumpkin for the base. This sauce mixed with pasta and topped with a buttery breadcrumb topping makes this an irresistible go-to meal to feed the family any night of the week. Don't be afraid to prep this ahead and have it mixed and topped with breadcrumbs in advance so you can just pop it in the oven for 30 minutes when you come home from work!

FOR THE PUNK CHEDDAH SAUCE

1½ cups (380 g) pumpkin puree

½ cup (68 g) raw cashews, soaked overnight or boiled in water for 10 minutes, drained and rinsed

¼ cup (24 g) nutritional yeast

2 tablespoons (42 g) white miso

3 cups (705 ml) water

1 tablespoon (15 g) Dijon mustard

1 tablespoon (15 ml) soy sauce or gluten-free tamari

1 tablespoon (20 g) maple syrup

Juice of ½ lemon

1½ teaspoons sea salt

1½ teaspoons onion powder

1½ teaspoons garlic powder

FOR THE BAKE

1 pound (454 g) elbow macaroni pasta

Cooking spray

2 tablespoons (28 g) vegan butter, melted

½ cup (25 g) panko or gluten-free panko breadcrumbs

Paprika (optional)

To make the punk cheddah sauce
Add the pumpkin, cashews, nutritional yeast, miso, water, Dijon mustard, soy sauce, maple syrup, lemon juice, salt, onion powder, and garlic powder to a blender. Blend for 1 to 2 minutes, until smooth and creamy.

To make the bake
Preheat the oven to 350°F (180°C, or gas mark 4). Lightly coat a 9 × 13-inch (23 × 33 cm) baking dish or 3-quart baking dish with cooking spray. Prepare the macaroni according to package directions.

Drain the pasta and return it to the pot. Mix in the sauce until all the pasta is coated and transfer it to the prepared baking dish.

Combine the melted butter and panko in a small bowl until the crumbs are coated completely. Sprinkle it over the top of the macaroni and cheese. Sprinkle with paprika (if using).

Bake for 30 to 35 minutes, until the edges of the macaroni and cheese just start to turn golden brown. Serve warm.

Note

Be extra epic and add an 8-ounce (227 g) bag of vegan cheddar shreds when mixing the sauce and pasta together.

Creamy Shiitake and Cauliflower Rice Risotto

YIELD: 4 SERVINGS

What a gift cauliflower rice has become when I'm trying to watch my calorie intake. It allows me to feel as though I'm having something truly decadent with the calories slashed right in half. This hearty cauliflower risotto gives you all the creamy goodness you want with crisp fresh veggies, and the perfect touch of umami flavor comes through from the sautéed shiitakes. Just be sure to prep your cream sauce and cauliflower rice before you turn on your heat. Even with that prep, this dish comes together easily in 30 minutes flat.

½ cup (120 ml) vegan sour cream

2 tablespoons (32 g) white miso paste

2 tablespoons (30 g) Dijon mustard

¾ teaspoon sea salt

½ teaspoon black pepper

2 tablespoons (28 g) vegan butter

1 onion, roughly chopped

5 ounces (140 g) shiitake mushrooms, sliced

1½ cups (225 g) frozen peas

4 cloves garlic, minced

4 cups (960 g) cauliflower rice

Chopped fresh parsley (optional)

Vegan parmesan (optional)

Crushed red pepper (optional)

Add the vegan sour cream, miso, Dijon mustard, salt, and pepper to a bowl. Whisk until well combined. Set aside.

Heat the butter in a large skillet over medium heat. Add the onion and mushrooms. Sauté for 4 to 6 minutes, until the onions are soft and the mushrooms have reduced in size. Add the peas and sauté for 2 minutes, until heated through. Add the garlic and sauté for 1 minute, until fragrant. Add the cream mixture and stir until everything is coated in the cream.

Add the cauliflower rice and mix until everything is well combined. Allow to cook for 2 minutes, until heated through, but do not overcook or the cauliflower will become soft and mushy. Garnish with parsley, vegan parmesan, and crushed red pepper (if using).

Note

This is very versatile. Add any vegetables you love! It's great in the summer with seasonal garden vegetables or in the fall with roasted squash. Just remember to cook the vegetables first and add the cauliflower last to keep the cauliflower from getting soggy or mushy, and you'll be all set!

Apricot Risotto

YIELD: 4 SERVINGS

If you're intimidated about the process of making risotto, don't be. It's really a cinch once you get the gist of it, and by the time all the additions have been made, you are left with deliciously tender and flavor-infused rice that is well worth the effort.

1 onion, chopped

½ cup (65 g) chopped dried apricots

¼ cup (60 ml) olive oil

Dash of black pepper

1 cup (190 g) Arborio rice

⅓ cup (80 ml) Chardonnay, warmed slightly above room temperature

3 to 4 cups (705 to 940 ml) vegetable broth, warmed

⅓ cup (80 ml) nondairy milk, warmed

1 tablespoon (14 g) nondairy margarine

Salt, to taste

Note

For dishes like this, I enjoy cooking with almond milk because it adds a very subtle flavor and does not curdle like soy milk tends to do.

In a large saucepan, sauté onion and apricots in the olive oil over medium heat, just until the onions turn translucent. Add a dash of pepper. Remove from the pan using a slotted spoon and place on a separate plate, leaving the oil in the pan.

Keeping the temperature at around medium heat, add the rice to the pan and cook for about 7 minutes or until the rice is golden brown, stirring occasionally. Add the wine and stir.

Reduce the heat slightly and let cook until all the wine has evaporated or been absorbed. Add the onions and apricots back into the pan and add a little vegetable broth. You just need enough to cover the rice, about ½ cup (120 ml) to start with.

Let the rice simmer in the broth over medium heat until almost all the liquid has been absorbed. Stir often to prevent sticking.

Add more broth and cook until there is just a little liquid left to be absorbed. Keep repeating this process. It should take about 25 minutes of adding liquid in increments and stirring until the rice is softened up. If you find that you are running out of liquid too fast, reduce the heat and add less liquid at each interval.

Add more broth and keep cooking if the rice is still too firm after 3 cups (705 ml) of broth have been added.

Once the rice is suitably cooked, stir in the nondairy milk and continue cooking until most of the liquid has been absorbed. It should look very creamy and the rice should be tender. Stir in the margarine.

Cover with a tight-fitting lid, turn off the heat, and let rest for about 10 minutes. Add salt to taste and serve.

Spicy Sushi Bowl

YIELD: 4 SERVINGS

Fluffy sushi rice, topped with fresh veggies, sweet mango, creamy avocado, and a homemade spicy sesame mayo, make up this easy-to-prepare sushi bowl. The edamame shines like little green gems and brings the protein, while the panko crumbs give it some crunch.

FOR THE SPICY MAYONNAISE

1 package (12 ounces [340 g]) soft silken tofu

¼ cup (60 ml) rice vinegar

¼ cup (60 ml) toasted sesame oil

3 tablespoons (45 ml) sriracha hot sauce

¾ teaspoon salt

¼ teaspoon garlic powder

½ teaspoon agave nectar

FOR THE SUSHI BOWL

1 cup (180 g) sushi rice

2 cups (475 ml) water

1 tablespoon (15 ml) rice vinegar

2 sheets of nori seaweed, cut into strips

4 ounces (115 g) cucumber, julienne-cut

6 ounces (170 g) daikon radish, julienne-cut

6 ounces (170 g) mango, peeled, seeded, and thinly sliced

1 cup (146 g) sliced avocado

1 cup (150 g) edamame, steamed and removed from pods

3 tablespoons (10 g) panko breadcrumbs (gluten-free, if necessary), toasted

1 tablespoon (8 g) sesame seeds, toasted

To make the spicy mayonnaise

Place all the ingredients in a food processor or blender and puree until completely smooth. Transfer the mayo to a jar or large squeeze bottle and store in the refrigerator for up to 3 weeks. (This recipe makes more than you will need for the sushi bowls.)

To make the sushi bowl

Place the sushi rice, water, and rice vinegar in a pot over medium-low heat, partially cover, and bring to a boil. Lower the heat and simmer for 20 to 25 minutes until the rice is soft, but not mushy. Fluff with a wooden spoon.

Divide the nori strips among 4 bowls, crisscrossing them. Divide the cooked rice among the bowls, as well as the cucumber, daikon radish, mango, avocado, and edamame. Combine the panko breadcrumbs and sesame seeds in a small bowl and then sprinkle the crunchies over each bowl. Finish each bowl with a drizzle of spicy mayo. Serve immediately.

Beany Burger Bowl

YIELD: 4 SERVINGS

Burgers can be awesome, but burger bowls are even better because you don't have to worry about adding so many toppings that you can't fit the burger into your mouth. Here's a delicious, basic beany burger bowl that has special sauce and quick pickles and can easily be embellished to suit your cravings.

**FOR THE
QUICK PICKLES**

3 ounces (90 ml) hot water

2 tablespoons (28 ml) white vinegar

1 teaspoon organic cane sugar

½ teaspoon dried dill

¼ teaspoon salt

1 small pickling cucumber, sliced into rounds

FOR THE SPECIAL SAUCE

¼ cup (60 g) vegan mayo

2 tablespoons (30 g) ketchup

2 tablespoons (30 g) relish

1½ tablespoons (17 g) yellow mustard

**FOR THE
BURGER PATTIES**

1 can (15 ounces [425 g]) kidney beans, rinsed and drained

1 cup (100 g) walnuts

1 tablespoon (16 g) tomato paste

1 tablespoon (15 ml) vegan Worcestershire sauce

1 tablespoon (15 ml) toasted sesame oil

1 teaspoon onion powder

1 teaspoon smoked sea salt

¼ teaspoon black pepper

FOR THE ASSEMBLY

12 butter lettuce leaves

2 thick slices of bread, cubed and toasted

1 cup (180 g) sliced tomatoes

½ cup (80 g) thinly sliced white onion

To make the quick pickles

In a small jar, stir the hot water, white vinegar, sugar, dill, and salt together until the sugar has dissolved. Add the cucumber slices to the jar, shake, and store in the refrigerator for at least 30 minutes.

To make the special sauce

In a small bowl, stir the mayo, ketchup, relish, and mustard together until combined. Place in the refrigerator for 30 minutes to chill before serving.

To make the burger patties

Preheat the oven to 350°F (180°C, or gas mark 4) and line a baking sheet with parchment paper.

Pulse the kidney beans and walnuts in a food processor until it is a crumbly mixture, but not a paste. Transfer to a bowl and fold the tomato paste, Worcestershire sauce, sesame oil, onion powder, smoked sea salt, and pepper into the kidney bean mixture until evenly combined. Form 8 burger patties, approximately ¾ inch (2 cm) thick, and place them on the baking sheet. Bake for 15 minutes and then flip them over and bake for an additional 10 minutes or until they begin to brown lightly. Place the baking sheet on a cooling rack for 5 minutes.

To assemble

Place 3 leaves of butter lettuce in each of the bowls and then divide the toasted bread cubes, tomato slices, and white onion among them. Add 2 burger patties to each bowl, top with pickles, and serve immediately with the special sauce.

Jackfruit Chili Verde

YIELD: 4 SERVINGS

Here is a meal that is about as "meat and potatoes" as you can get while remaining vegan. Seasoned jackfruit is used in place of meat, while potatoes add body to a spicy tomatillo and chile pepper base.

1 tablespoon (15 ml) olive oil

½ cup (80 g) diced white onion

2 cloves garlic, minced

1 can (20 ounces [560 g]) young jackfruit in brine, drained

1 teaspoon dried oregano

1 teaspoon ground cumin

½ teaspoon ground coriander

4 Anaheim chile peppers

½ pound (225 g) tomatillos, husks removed

1 serrano chile pepper

1 fresh jalapeño

3 cups (700 ml) gluten-free vegetable broth

1½ pounds (680 g) russet potatoes, peeled and chopped

2 teaspoons salt, or to taste

⅛ teaspoon black pepper, or to taste

1 tablespoon (1 g) fresh cilantro leaves

Prepare a hot fire in a grill (375°F, or 190°C) and oil the grill grates.

In a large pot, heat the olive oil over medium heat. Add the onion and sauté until translucent. Next, add the garlic, jackfruit, oregano, cumin, and coriander, breaking the jackfruit apart with a wooden spoon while browning it. Cook for 6 to 8 minutes until the jackfruit has reduced in size and browned.

Place the Anaheim chiles, tomatillos, serrano chile, and jalapeño on the grill. Grill until charred on all sides and then place on a plate and cover with a larger plate or a bowl to steam off the skins. Wait 5 minutes before removing the skins, stems, and seeds from the peppers. Put the tomatillos and peppers into a blender, along with the vegetable broth, pureeing until smooth.

Add the chile mixture and potatoes to the pot and bring to a boil. Adjust the heat to medium-low and simmer, partially covered, for 25 minutes or until the potatoes are fork-tender. Season with the salt and pepper and serve garnished with the cilantro.

Note

To add more protein to this meal, use 8 ounces (225 g) steamed tempeh or pressed and cubed tofu in place of or in addition to the jackfruit; prepare it in the same manner as the jackfruit. Note that the recipe will no longer be soy-free with the addition of tofu or tempeh.

Upside-Down Shepherd's Pie

YIELD: 4 SERVINGS

Imagine it's a rainy, cold, dreary day and all you want to do is to cozy up to a warm meal. What will you be making? This upside-down shepherd's pie, of course! Mashed potatoes topped with hearty potpie filling will satisfy you without the long oven baking time.

FOR THE MASHED POTATOES

2 pounds (910 g) russet potatoes, peeled and chopped

3 cups (700 ml) vegetable broth

½ cup (120 ml) unsweetened nondairy milk (gluten-free, if necessary)

2 tablespoons (28 g) coconut oil

1 teaspoon salt, or to taste

FOR THE "FILLING"

1 tablespoon (14 g) coconut oil

1½ cups (134 g) sliced leeks

1 large carrot, sliced into coins

1 stalk of celery, chopped

½ pound (225 g) button mushrooms, sliced

½ cup (154 g) corn kernels

½ cup (75 g) peas

1 tablespoon (4 g) nutritional yeast

1 tablespoon (8 g) chickpea flour

1 tablespoon (15 ml) vegan Worcestershire sauce (gluten-free, if necessary)

5 sprigs of fresh thyme, plus more for garnish

¼ teaspoon ground sage

½ teaspoon salt, or to taste

Pinch of black pepper

To make the mashed potatoes

Place the potatoes and vegetable broth in a large pot, adding water until the potatoes are covered. Bring to a boil over medium heat and then adjust the heat to medium-low, cover, and cook for 15 to 20 minutes until the potatoes are fork-tender.

Drain the potatoes, reserving 1 cup (235 ml) of the broth, and return them to the pot. Add the nondairy milk, coconut oil, and salt, mashing until slightly chunky. Cover to keep warm.

To make the "filling"

In a large skillet, melt the coconut oil over medium heat. Sauté the leeks, carrot, and celery in the oil for 5 minutes, stirring occasionally. Next, add the mushrooms, corn, and peas, sautéing for 5 to 7 minutes, until the mushrooms have reduced in size. Stir in the nutritional yeast, chickpea flour, and vegan Worcestershire sauce.

Pour the reserved vegetable broth into the skillet, stirring until evenly combined. Add the thyme and sage and simmer for 10 minutes or until the mixture has thickened and the carrots are tender. Season with the salt and pepper.

Divide the mashed potatoes among 4 bowls, topping each mound with the "filling" and 2 sprigs of fresh thyme. Serve immediately.

"Fish" Taco Bowl

YIELD: 4 SERVINGS

Taco Tuesday is a weekly holiday that I celebrate regularly, and for good reason—tacos are freakin' awesome! I will admit, however, that sometimes I'm not into getting my hands dirty from tortillas bursting at the seams with fillings, so this taco bowl is a great alternative.

FOR THE CABBAGE SLAW

1 cup (70 g) shredded red cabbage

1 cup (70 g) shredded green cabbage

1 cup (110 g) grated carrot

¼ cup (60 g) vegan mayonnaise (soy-free, if necessary)

1 teaspoon white vinegar

FOR THE PICO DE GALLO

½ cup (90 g) diced tomatoes

⅓ cup (55 g) diced red onion

1 tablespoon (1 g) minced fresh cilantro

1 tablespoon (6 g) minced fresh jalapeño (optional)

½ teaspoon lime juice

Salt and black pepper, to taste

FOR THE "FISH"

2 cans (14 ounces [400 g] each) hearts of palm, drained

2 teaspoons lime juice

½ teaspoon dulse seaweed flakes

Pinch of salt

FOR THE ASSEMBLY

4 small corn tortillas, cut into strips

¼ cup (4 g) loosely packed fresh cilantro leaves

2 tablespoons (11 g) sliced fresh jalapeño

8 lime wedges

To make the cabbage slaw
Place all the ingredients in a bowl, stir together until combined, and then refrigerate for 20 minutes.

To make the pico de gallo
Place all the ingredients in a bowl, stir together until combined, and then refrigerate for 20 minutes.

To make the "fish"
Preheat the oven to 350°F (180°C, or gas mark 4) and coat a baking sheet with a thin layer of oil or nonstick cooking spray.

In a mixing bowl, using 2 forks or your hands, pull apart the hearts of palm until they appear shredded. Stir in the lime juice, dulse flakes, and salt until combined and then spread the mixture out on the baking sheet in a single layer. Bake for 12 to 15 minutes until the edges start to turn golden brown.

To assemble
While the "fish" is baking, place the tortilla strips on a baking sheet, brush with a thin layer of oil, and sprinkle with salt. Bake for 10 to 12 minutes until crispy.

Divide the slaw, pico de gallo, "fish," and tortillas among 4 shallow bowls, arranging the components in quadrants. Nestle the cilantro, jalapeño, and lime wedges in with the tortilla strips. Serve immediately.

Asparagus and Mushroom Tacos with Cilantro Mayonnaise

YIELD: 12 TACOS

Taco night is always a favorite in our house, and we like to mix it up as often as possible. These feature asparagus and mushrooms and are an absolutely delicious way to spice up your evening meal. Try to find corn tortillas made from just corn, salt, and maybe a little lime juice, such as Trader Joe's brand.

FOR THE FILLING

16 ounces (450 g) cremini mushrooms, thinly sliced

1 to 3 serrano chile peppers (depending on your heat level preference), stemmed, seeded, and minced

3 cloves garlic, minced

1 small onion, diced

2 teaspoons cumin

1 to 2 teaspoons red chile powder

¼ teaspoon chipotle chile powder

1 teaspoon minced fresh thyme leaves

1 teaspoon salt

2 tablespoons (30 ml) canola oil, divided

8 stalks asparagus, tough ends removed

FOR THE CILANTRO MAYONNAISE

⅓ cup (5 g) finely chopped fresh cilantro

1 tablespoon (15 ml) lime juice

1 cup (225 g) vegan mayonnaise

FOR SERVING

12 corn tortillas

½ cup (8 g) chopped fresh cilantro

1 cup (150 g) diced fresh tomatoes

To make the filling

In a large frying pan, toss together the mushrooms, serrano chiles, garlic, onion, cumin, red chile powder, chipotle powder, thyme, salt, and 1½ tablespoons (22 ml) of the oil. Cover and cook over medium heat, stirring occasionally, until the mushrooms are tender and have released a good amount of liquid, about 10 minutes. Uncover and reduce the heat to low. Simmer until all the liquid is gone, approximately 7 minutes longer.

Slice the asparagus stalks in half down the length of the spear. Place in a separate frying pan with the remaining ½ tablespoon (8 ml) oil. Sauté over medium-high heat for 2 to 3 minutes or until bright green and tender. Set aside.

To make the cilantro mayonnaise

Mix all the ingredients together until well combined.

To serve

Using a flat skillet or cast-iron pan, warm the tortillas gently on each side until pliable and light golden brown. As each tortilla cooks, stack in a pile and cover with foil to retain heat and moisture.

Assemble the tacos by first adding the mushroom mixture, then the asparagus, then a little fresh cilantro, a few chopped tomatoes, and finally, the cilantro mayonnaise.

Jackfruit Tacos with Black Beans

YIELD: 5 SERVINGS

California has the best and most accessible Mexican food outside of Mexico, hands down, which meant growing up in Southern California had some serious food perks. These tacos are reminiscent of the street tacos from the food trucks I would ride my bike to. Of course, I had to round them out with a side of seasoned black beans!

FOR THE TACOS

3 cans (14 ounces [400 g]) young jackfruit in brine, drained, rinsed, and seeded

1 tablespoon (15 ml) sunflower oil

1½ teaspoons ancho chile powder

1 teaspoon dried oregano

½ teaspoon onion powder

¼ cup (60 ml) water

1½ tablespoons (25 ml) tamari or coconut aminos

1 tablespoon (15 ml) maple syrup

FOR THE BEANS

2 cans (15 ounces [425 g]) low-sodium black beans, liquid reserved

3 bay leaves

1 teaspoon ground cumin

1 teaspoon onion powder

½ teaspoon garlic powder

¼ to ½ teaspoon salt

FOR THE ASSEMBLY

10 small corn tortillas

1½ cups (118 g) shredded green cabbage

½ cup (70 g) diced white onion

¼ cup (4 g) chopped cilantro, loosely packed

2 radishes, quartered and sliced thin

5 lime wedges

To make the tacos

Pull apart any large pieces of jackfruit. In a large skillet, heat the oil over medium heat. Add the jackfruit, ancho chile powder, oregano, and onion powder and cook until the jackfruit is browned and dry and the edges are crispy, 5 to 7 minutes.

Add the water, tamari, and maple syrup and continue to cook until the liquid has been soaked up and the edges of the jackfruit start to sizzle. Turn heat to low to keep warm (or remove from heat if storing).

To make the beans

While the jackfruit is cooking, simmer the beans and their liquid, bay leaves, cumin, onion powder, garlic powder, and salt over medium-low heat, with a vented lid, until warmed through, about 10 minutes. Remove and discard the bay leaves.

To assemble

Divide the beans among 5 small storage containers (or the small sections of 5 partitioned storage containers). Warm the tortillas by toasting them 1 at a time over a gas burner or microwaving the stack for 30 seconds. Place 2 tortillas in each of 5 large storage containers (or the large section of the partitioned containers), and divide jackfruit evenly among tortillas. Top the jackfruit with cabbage, onion, cilantro, and radishes and place lime wedges on the side. Tacos can be stored in the refrigerator for up to 5 days.

Sunny Garden Sauté with Polenta

YIELD: 4 SERVINGS

Growing your own food has its own rewards, but when that is not a possibility, going to the farmers' market is the next best thing. Walking along the rows of tents, looking at the wide variety of colorful produce—especially during the summer—and having the aroma of fresh herbs, tomatoes, and more waft by you is tantalizing. This bowl embodies all that goodness.

FOR THE GARDEN SAUTÉ

1 teaspoon olive oil

3 shallots, sliced

6 ounces (170 g) green beans, ends trimmed and chopped

1 small head radicchio, chopped

¼ pound (115 g) Swiss chard, chopped

1 pound (455 g) tomatoes, chopped

1 can (15 ounces [425 g]) white beans, rinsed and drained

½ teaspoon dried Italian seasoning

1 teaspoon salt, or to taste

¼ teaspoon black pepper, or to taste

FOR THE POLENTA

3 cups (700 ml) gluten-free vegetable broth

1 cup (140 g) polenta grits (I use Bob's Red Mill.)

Salt, to taste

To make the garden sauté

In a large skillet over medium heat, heat the olive oil. Sauté the shallots for 2 minutes and then add the green beans and cook for 5 minutes, stirring occasionally. (During this time, get started on the polenta.)

Add the radicchio, Swiss chard, tomatoes, white beans, and Italian seasoning to the skillet and sauté until the greens become wilted. Season with the salt and pepper.

To make the polenta

In a large pot over medium heat, bring the vegetable broth to a boil. Stir the polenta into the broth, adjust the heat to medium-low, and cook until the polenta is soft and creamy, about 15 to 20 minutes. Season with salt.

Divide the polenta among 4 bowls, top with the garden sauté, and serve.

Raw Crunch Bowl

YIELD: 4 SERVINGS

Spiralizing vegetables into noodles is something I love to do when I am looking to have a healthy, easy meal with tons of crunch to it. These mixed veggie noodles are slathered in a creamy almond and red pepper sauce and topped with raw salted almonds.

FOR THE CREAMY PEPPER SAUCE

½ cup (73 g) raw almonds, soaked in warm water for 2 hours, drained, and peeled

2 cups (300 g) chopped red bell pepper

¼ cup (60 ml) water

1 tablespoon (15 ml) apple cider vinegar

1 clove garlic, peeled

½ teaspoon salt

¼ teaspoon black pepper

FOR THE ALMOND TOPPING

½ cup (73 g) raw almonds, soaked in warm water for 2 hours and peeled

¼ teaspoon salt

Pinch of black pepper

FOR THE VEGGIE NOODLES

½ pound (225 g) zucchini, sliced on a spiralizer

½ pound (225 g) yellow squash, sliced on a spiralizer

¼ pound (115 g) rainbow carrots, sliced on a spiralizer

Fresh basil leaves, for garnish

To make the creamy pepper sauce

In a blender, place all the ingredients and puree until very smooth. Set aside.

To make the almond topping

Chop the almonds, place them in a small bowl, and toss with the salt and pepper.

To make the veggie noodles

In a large bowl, toss the different vegetable noodles together and then divide them among 4 large bowls. Drizzle the creamy pepper sauce over each bowl, finish with the almond topping and a couple of basil leaves, and serve.

Note

Here's a fun way to peel almonds: Once they are soaked and drained, squeeze them between your thumb and index finger at the round end of the nut. The almond will quite easily shoot out of the skin through the pointy end.

Kimchi Bowl with Red Curry Almond Sauce

YIELD: 4 SERVINGS

Kimchi is not only extremely tasty, but its probiotic qualities also help your gut health. In this bowl, the kimchi is nestled among brown rice, broccoli, adzuki beans, and a spicy red curry almond sauce; it's a flavor explosion!

FOR THE BOWL

1 cup (184 g) long-grain brown rice

2 cups (245 ml) water

½ pound (225 g) broccoli florets

1 can (15 ounces [425 g]) adzuki beans, rinsed and drained

1 tablespoon (15 ml) liquid aminos

FOR THE RED CURRY ALMOND SAUCE

2½ tablespoons (38 ml) water

2 tablespoons (32 g) almond butter

2 teaspoons red curry paste

1 to 2 tablespoons (15 to 20 ml) lime juice

FOR THE ASSEMBLY

1 cup (170 g) store-bought vegan kimchi

2 tablespoons (16 g) black sesame seeds

To make the bowl

Place the rice and water in a rice cooker (that has a steamer basket) and cook for 20 minutes or until the rice is soft. For the last 5 minutes of the rice cooking, place the broccoli florets in the steamer basket and cook until bright green and slightly crunchy.

In a small pot over medium heat, mix the adzuki beans with the liquid aminos and cook for 2 to 3 minutes.

To make the red curry almond sauce

Whisk all the ingredients together until smooth.

To assemble

Divide the rice and broccoli among 4 bowls. Divide the adzuki beans among the bowls. Place one-quarter of the kimchi in each bowl and drizzle the red curry almond sauce over the top. Garnish with the black sesame seeds and serve.

Cold Sesame Noodles

YIELD: 6 SERVINGS

Inspired by a favorite dish often found in Chinese restaurants, these noodles are best when dressed with sauce and eaten immediately because the sauce soaks into the noodles so quickly. If you'd like to make ahead of time, simply store the sauce and noodles separately and combine just before serving.

16 ounces mỹ tho noodles (flat, wide Asian rice noodles) or other long, wide rice noodles

2 cubes (2 teaspoons) vegetable bouillon

2 tablespoons Bragg's liquid aminos, plus extra to douse noodles

2 tablespoons (32 g) smooth peanut butter

3 tablespoons (45 ml) toasted sesame oil

2 tablespoons (30 ml) agave nectar

½ teaspoon turmeric

1 teaspoon cumin

1 teaspoon Chinese five-spice powder

1 teaspoon freshly grated ginger

¼ cup (25 g) chopped scallion, for garnish

Toasted black sesame seeds, for garnish

Chili garlic sauce, such as sriracha, for serving

Cook the noodles according to the package directions, dissolving the bouillon cubes in the cooking water first. Once cooked, transfer the noodles to a colander and toss with cold water until they are easy to handle and any extra starch has been rinsed away. Drain well and liberally toss with Bragg's liquid aminos, covering evenly until the noodles appear a golden brown all over.

In a separate bowl, combine the peanut butter and sesame oil and stir until smooth. Stir in the 2 tablespoons (30 ml) Bragg's, agave, turmeric, cumin, Chinese five-spice powder, and ginger. Pour over the noodles and toss until they are completely covered with a thin layer of sauce.

Garnish with scallion and sesame seeds. You can add the hot sauce on top, stir it in to taste, or pass at the table. Refrigerate for about 30 minutes before serving, tossing occasionally to keep moist. Serve cold.

Slow-Simmered Tofu with Peanut Sauce

YIELD: 4 SERVINGS

This savory tofu dish requires a little forethought because you need to freeze the tofu overnight and simmer the dish for some time, but it's well worth it. The peanut sauce lends just the right amount of sweetness to the dish and is also great served over basmati rice or quinoa.

1 package (15 ounces [425 g]) extra-firm tofu

5 carrots, peeled and sliced

2 cans (13.5 ounces [378 g] each) full-fat coconut milk

1 medium-size Spanish onion, diced

2 cloves garlic, minced

1 teaspoon freshly grated ginger

3 bay leaves

¼ cup (65 g) creamy peanut butter

⅛ teaspoon mombasa powder, or ¼ teaspoon cayenne pepper

Salt, to taste

Cooked basmati rice, for serving

The night before you begin, drain and press the tofu, cut into 4 equal pieces, and seal tightly in a freezer-safe plastic bag. Freeze overnight.

The next day, in a large, heavy skillet, stir together the sliced carrots, coconut milk, onion, garlic, ginger, bay leaves, peanut butter, and mombasa. Place the frozen tofu cutlets (no need to thaw) in the pan, shimmying the tofu down into the coconut mixture while gently guiding the veggies to the sides of the tofu so that the cutlets lie flat in the pan.

Cook over medium heat until the sauce begins to boil, about 15 minutes. Cover, reduce the heat to medium-low, and simmer for about 2 hours, spooning sauce on top of the tofu every once in a while. During the duration of the cooking time, do not flip over the cutlets! You want them to get nice and caramelized on the bottom side, so let them stay right where they are the entire cooking time. Stir the sauce occasionally.

Uncover the pan and cook for 1 hour longer or until the sauce has reduced to a thick, gravy-like consistency and the edges of the carrots and onions are golden brown. The total cooking time is 3 hours. Remove the bay leaves, add salt to taste, and serve over some fluffy basmati rice.

Note

Mombasa is a chile pepper (in the cayenne family) that packs a lot of heat! It is said to be one of the hottest spices available and is often used in African cuisine. It is not all that common and is usually found only in specialty spice stores. Cayenne pepper can be substituted in place; just double the amount!

Stroganoff

YIELD: 6 SERVINGS

Stroganoff was one of my faves as a youngster, even though I seemed to always avoid eating the beef tips. This recipe holds the same great flavor I remember, but it's animal-free!

¼ cup (60 ml) olive oil, divided

1 Vidalia onion, chopped

20 ounces (175 g) sliced cremini or button mushrooms

Salt, to taste

1 cup (235 ml) boiling water mixed with 2 beef-flavored bouillon cubes, or 1 cup (235 ml) concentrated vegetable broth

1¾ cups (420 ml) canned full-fat coconut milk, divided

1 tablespoon (15 ml) wheat-free vegan Worcestershire sauce (or wheat-free tamari)

1 to 3 tablespoons (8 to 24 g) sorghum flour, divided

1 teaspoon black pepper, plus a dash or two

12 ounces (340 g) brown rice pasta spirals or flat, wide white rice Asian-style noodles

Black pepper, to taste

Heat 1 tablespoon (15 ml) of the oil in a large skillet and add the onion and mushrooms. Cook over medium-to-high heat until the onions begin to brown and caramelize. Salt lightly. The mushrooms will produce a good deal of water as they cook. Continue cooking until almost all the water has cooked out of them and the onions are translucent, about 10 minutes. Reduce the heat to low.

In a small heat-proof bowl, combine the boiling water and bouillon cubes, stirring to dissolve. Add to the mushrooms and onions. Add 1 cup (235 ml) of the coconut milk and let simmer for about 20 minutes, stirring occasionally.

Add the remaining ¾ cup (185 ml) coconut milk, Worcestershire sauce, 1 tablespoon (8 g) of the sorghum flour, and 1 teaspoon pepper. Whisk together vigorously until very smooth, making sure there are no lumps of sorghum lingering in the sauce. Cook over medium-high heat, stirring continuously, until thickened, about 7 minutes. Whisk in some or all the remaining 2 tablespoons (16 g) sorghum flour if needed to thicken even more. Add salt to taste.

Cook the noodles in a large pot of salted, boiling water for about 5 minutes or following the package directions. Drain and rinse briefly under cold water. Return the noodles to the pot and toss with the remaining 3 tablespoons (45 ml) olive oil, a dash or two more pepper, and a touch of salt to taste.

Combine the mushroom sauce with the noodles while both are still hot. Top with black pepper and serve.

Black Bean, Potato, and Cheese Enchiladas

YIELD: 12 ENCHILADAS

The key to keeping the tortillas from splitting while rolling is to use the freshest and best-quality corn tortillas you can find. Generally they should just include corn, salt, and maybe a touch of lime juice. I always have luck locating these at Mexican groceries or even at Trader Joe's and recommend sourcing your tortillas there if you have one nearby.

FOR THE ENCHILADA SAUCE

1 cup (240 g) diced canned tomatoes, drained

1 can (8 ounces [225 g]) tomato sauce

½ to 1 teaspoon sea salt

3 dried chile peppers (guajillos or chipotles)

2 cloves garlic, minced

1 tablespoon (7 g) cumin

1 tablespoon (15 ml) olive oil

2 cups (470 ml) vegetable broth

¼ cup (40 g) minced red onion

1 can (6 ounces [170 g]) tomato paste

FOR THE ENCHILADAS

2 cups (220 g) diced potatoes (dice small for faster cooking)

1 tablespoon (15 ml) olive oil

Dash or two of salt

12 corn tortillas

1 can (15 ounces [420 g]) black beans, drained

2 cups (230 g) nondairy shredded cheese, such as Daiya brand pepper jack

To make the enchilada sauce

Combine all the sauce ingredients in a saucepan and simmer over medium heat until the chile peppers are plump and rehydrated, about 20 minutes. Let cool and then process in a blender until very smooth.

To make the enchiladas

Over medium-high heat, sauté the potatoes in olive oil with the salt until lightly golden brown, stirring often to prevent sticking. Remove from the heat and let cool briefly.

Preheat the oven to 350°F (180°C, or gas mark 4) and lightly grease a 9 × 13-inch (23 × 33 cm) baking dish.

Pour about ½ cup (120 ml) of the enchilada sauce onto a large rimmed plate or bowl. Have the rest of your ingredients, plus a large clean plate, lined up to assemble the enchiladas.

Dip 1 corn tortilla into the sauce, ensuring both front and back are completely covered with sauce. Transfer the single tortilla to a clean plate and fill with about 2 tablespoons (28 g) each of cooked potatoes, black beans, and cheese. Roll up to close and place in the baking dish seam side down. Repeat until all the tortillas are dipped, filled, and rolled, tucking each enchilada snugly into the

baking dish. The proximity of the enchiladas should be enough to keep them from unrolling. Cover the enchiladas with the remaining sauce and sprinkle with any remaining cheese, if desired.

Bake, uncovered, for about 20 minutes or until the tortillas become slightly crispy on top. Serve hot.

Lemon-Rosemary Chickpea Pasta Casserole

YIELD: 5 SERVINGS

I almost never make pasta casseroles—with the exception of mac and cheese—but this recipe has me asking myself, "Why the heck not?" Easy to prepare, lemony, herby, and downright comforting, this chickpea and pasta casserole delivers on all fronts!

2 teaspoons (10 ml) sunflower oil

1 cup (140 g) diced yellow onion

1 cup (130 g) diced carrot

1 cup (100 g) diced celery

2 cans (15 ounces [425 g]) chickpeas, drained, with 1 cup (235 ml) liquid reserved

1 cup (137 g) raw cashews

¼ cup (60 ml) lemon juice plus 1 tablespoon (6 g) zest

3 cloves garlic, peeled

2 teaspoons (2 g) dried rosemary

1 teaspoon salt

½ teaspoon black pepper

4 cups (280 g) bowtie pasta, gluten-free if desired

4 cups (950 ml) hot vegetable broth or vegan chicken broth

Preheat the oven to 375°F (190°C, or gas mark 5). In a large skillet, heat the oil over medium heat. Add the onion, carrot, and celery and cook until the onions are close to translucent, about 5 minutes. Add the chickpeas and cook for another 2 minutes.

While the veggie mixture is cooking, puree the chickpea liquid, cashews, lemon juice and zest, garlic, rosemary, salt, and pepper in a blender until very smooth. Let sit for 2 minutes, then blend again.

Pour the pasta, hot broth, chickpea mixture, and blended sauce into a 9 × 13-inch (23 × 33 cm) casserole dish. Stir to combine and spread mixture into an even layer. Cover the dish with foil and bake for 30 minutes. Carefully remove the foil and bake until the pasta is cooked through and the sauce is no longer runny, about 10 minutes longer. Let cool on a rack for 15 minutes before serving. Casserole can be stored in the refrigerator for up to 7 days or in the freezer for up to 3 months.

Note

If you want to dress this dish up looks-wise, top it with a few sprigs of rosemary during the last 10 minutes of baking.

Mushroom Onion Burgers

YIELD: 4 SERVINGS

You gotta love a good veggie burger! Except for when they're a mushy mess—no thank you. These burgers have great texture and are never mushy, thanks to the mixture of walnuts, oats, beans, and mushrooms. Plus, the sautéed topping just takes it to another level.

½ cup (50 g) raw walnuts

½ cup (45 g) quick-cooking oats

1 teaspoon smoked paprika

1 teaspoon onion powder

1 teaspoon dried parsley

¼ teaspoon black pepper, plus more to taste

1 large yellow onion, sliced into rings, divided

1 can (15 ounces [425 g]) kidney beans, drained and rinsed

6 ounces (170 g) sliced cremini mushrooms, divided

1 tablespoon (15 ml) olive oil

1 tablespoon (15 ml) tamari or coconut aminos

½ teaspoon salt, plus more to taste

1 tablespoon (15 ml) sunflower oil

1 tablespoon (15 ml) red wine or water

4 slices vegan provolone or smoked gouda (optional)

4 burger buns, gluten-free if desired

2 cups (40 g) baby arugula

Preheat the oven to 375°F (190°C, or gas mark 5) and line a baking sheet with parchment paper. Pulse the walnuts, oats, smoked paprika, onion powder, dried parsley, and ¼ teaspoon pepper in a food processor equipped with an S-blade until the walnuts are fine crumbles. Dice ½ cup (60 g) of the onion rings and add to the processor along with the beans, ½ cup (40 g) of the mushrooms, the olive oil, the tamari, and ½ teaspoon salt. Pulse until it forms a dough, being careful not to overprocess into a paste.

Form the mixture into 4 patties, roughly 4 inches (10 cm) wide and ½ inch (1 cm) thick. Place them on the prepared baking sheet and bake for 20 minutes, then flip the patties and bake for another 15 minutes.

Meanwhile, heat the sunflower oil in a sauté pan over medium heat. Add the remaining onions and cook until the onions are translucent and beginning to brown on the edges, about 7 minutes. Reduce the heat to medium-low, add the remaining mushrooms and a pinch of salt to release their moisture, and cook for 10 minutes, stirring occasionally. Deglaze the pan with the wine and simmer for 2 more minutes. Season with salt and pepper to taste.

When the burgers are done, top each one with a slice of vegan cheese, if using, and place on bottom buns. Top with the mushroom mixture, arugula, and, lastly, the top buns. Serve immediately or store in the refrigerator for up to 5 days in airtight containers.

Note

If you're not eating these right away, prep the patties, bake them for 20 minutes, then take them out of the oven and let them cool to room temperature. Then, store them in an airtight container layered with pieces of wax paper in the freezer for up to 3 months.

Almond Butter Tofu Stew

YIELD: 4 SERVINGS

What's this? Almond butter stew? Why, yes! This recipe was inspired by west African groundnut stews, but I opted for the peanut-free route. And of course I added kale too, because I'm me, and we could all use a little more kale in our lives.

FOR THE RICE

2 cups (475 ml) water

1 cup (185 g) long-grain white rice, rinsed

FOR THE STEW

2 teaspoons (10 ml) sunflower oil

2 cups (240 g) chopped yellow onion

1 cup (150 g) chopped red bell pepper, stem and seeds removed

1 package (14 ounces [395 g]) extra-firm tofu, cut into ¾-inch (2 cm) cubes

1 pound (455 g) sweet potatoes, washed well and chopped

1 cup (160 g) chopped tomatoes

1 tablespoon (8 g) grated fresh ginger

3 cloves garlic, minced

½ cup (165 g) smooth almond butter

¼ cup (64 g) tomato paste

½ teaspoon ground coriander

⅛ teaspoon cayenne pepper, optional

3 cups (710 ml) vegetable broth

4 bay leaves

1 cup (40 g) firmly packed chopped kale

Salt, to taste

¼ cup (4 g) loosely packed cilantro leaves

4 lime wedges

Note

If you're allergic to almonds, use sunflower butter.

To make the rice

In a medium pot, bring the water and rice to a boil. Adjust the heat to medium-low and simmer, covered, until all the liquid is absorbed and the grains are fluffy, 15 to 20 minutes. Remove the pot from the heat, fluff the rice with a fork, and leave the lid vented.

To make the stew

While the rice is cooking, heat the oil in a large pot over medium heat. Add the onion and bell pepper and cook until the onion starts to soften, about 3 minutes. Push the onion mixture to the side of the pot and add the tofu to the empty space. Cook for 3 minutes, stirring occasionally, then stir in the sweet potatoes, tomatoes, ginger, and garlic and cook, covered, for another 5 minutes.

Add the almond butter, tomato paste, coriander, and cayenne, if using, stirring until evenly combined. Stir in the vegetable broth, add the bay leaves, cover the pot, and bring to a boil. Adjust the heat to medium-low and simmer until the sweet potatoes are easily pierced with a fork, about 15 minutes.

Remove the pot from the heat and discard the bay leaves. Stir in the kale and let it wilt for 1 to 2 minutes. Season with salt to taste. Divide the stew into 4 bowls or storage containers and serve with cilantro and lime wedges. The stew and rice can be stored in the refrigerator for up to 5 days or in the freezer for up to 3 months.

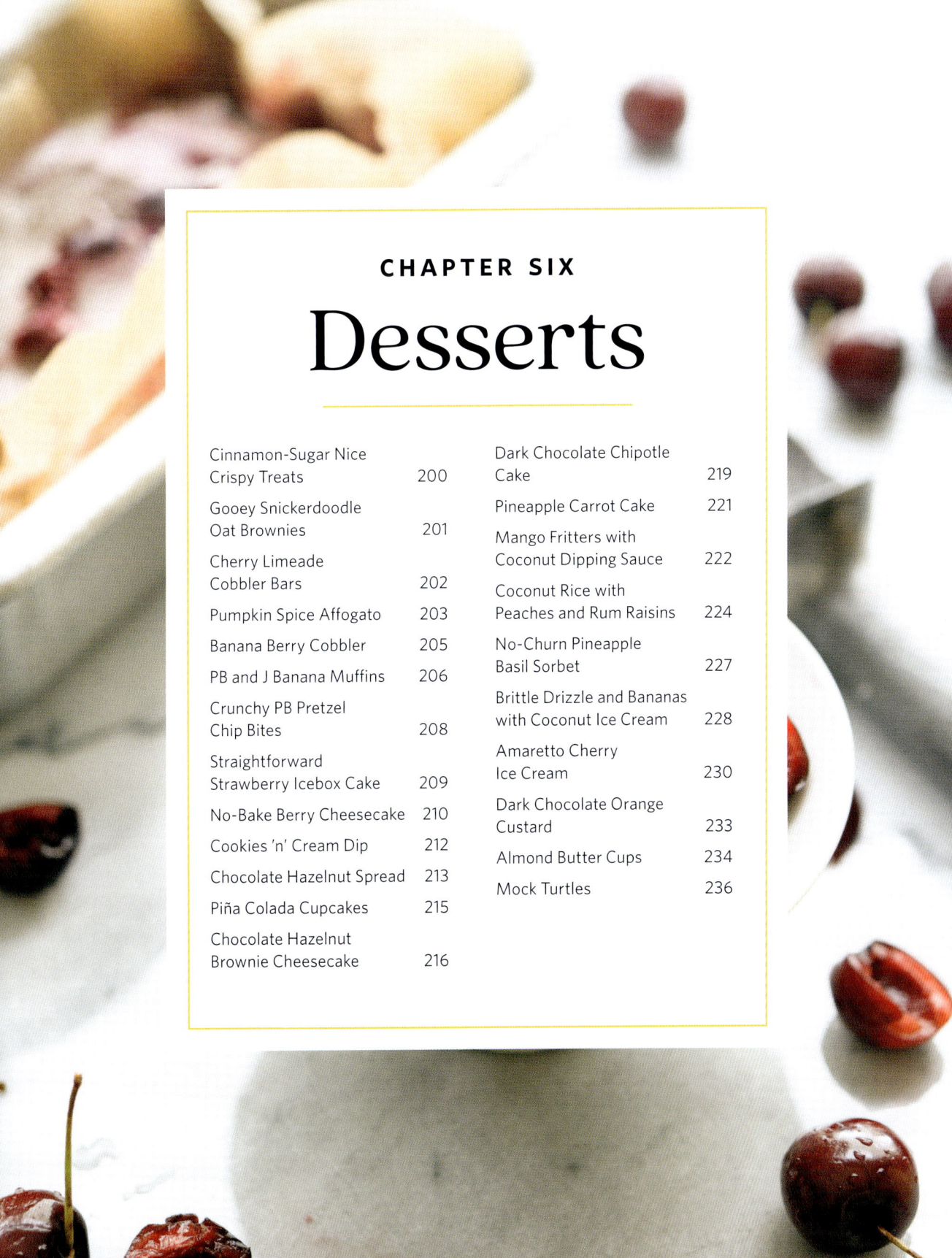

Desserts

Cinnamon-Sugar Nice Crispy Treats

YIELD: 12 SQUARES

We know these treats, and we love these treats! Thank heavens for brands like Dandies Marshmallows, who have been offering up vegan marshmallows since 2009. Fluffy, puffy, sweet, delicious, and all vegan. These treats have just a little extra added touch of cinnamon sugar, always a crowd-pleaser!

1 tablespoon (13 g) organic cane sugar

2 teaspoons (5 g) ground cinnamon, divided

Cooking spray

¼ cup (55 g) vegan butter

1 bag (10 ounces [283 g]) vegan mini marshmallows

5 cups (750 g) crispy rice cereal

In a small bowl, combine the sugar and 1 teaspoon cinnamon. Set aside.

Spray an 8 × 8-inch (20 × 20 cm) baking dish with cooking spray.

Add the butter and remaining cinnamon to a large saucepan and melt over medium-low heat. Add the marshmallows, stirring constantly, until melted. Remove from the heat and quickly add the cereal to the saucepan. Stir until all pieces are equally coated.

Coat a spatula with cooking spray. Transfer the mixture to the prepared baking dish using the prepared spatula (or your hands) and press the mixture into the baking dish until the top is flat and even. Sprinkle generously with cinnamon-sugar mixture.

Let cool completely and cut into 12 squares.

Note

Mix in your favorite extras! Add chocolate chips, dried cranberries, dried cherries, pistachios, cocoa powder, or whatever your little heart desires! These treats are a great canvas to customize to your taste or surprise someone on a special occasion by adding one of their favorite ingredients.

Gooey Snickerdoodle Oat Brownies

YIELD: 9 SQUARES

I've always loved snickerdoodle cookies. This is just a little twist on a favorite! This dessert is a fun one to put together with kids. It has the sweet and cinnamony delight of a cookie with the added swirl of butter, sugar, and oat crumble that creates gooey cracks in the brownie as it bakes. Try to eat just one.

Cooking spray

1 cup (125 g) all purpose or gluten-free all-purpose flour

1½ teaspoons baking powder

1 teaspoon sea salt, divided

2 teaspoons (5 g) cinnamon, divided

¾ cup (150 g) organic cane sugar

½ cup (120 ml) unsweetened soy or almond milk

2 tablespoons (30 ml) canola oil

1 teaspoon vanilla

2 tablespoons (28 g) vegan butter, melted

¼ cup (24 g) gluten-free rolled oats

¾ cup (113 g) light brown sugar

Preheat the oven to 350°F (180°C, or gas mark 4). Line an 8 × 8-inch (20 × 20 cm) baking dish with 2 inches (5 cm) of parchment paper with paper overhanging on 2 sides and lightly spray with cooking spray.

In a large bowl, whisk together the flour, baking powder, ½ teaspoon salt, 1 teaspoon cinnamon, sugar, milk, canola oil, and vanilla until smooth. Transfer to the prepared baking dish.

In a small bowl, combine the butter, rolled oats, brown sugar, remaining salt, and remaining cinnamon. Sprinkle the mixture over the top of the batter.

Bake in the oven for 45 minutes, until the top appears dry. Let cool completely. Pull the entire brownie out of the pan using the overhanging sides of the parchment paper and transfer to a cutting board. Cut into 9 squares.

Note

Mix in your favorite extras! Add chocolate chips, dried cranberries, dried cherries, pistachios, cocoa powder, or whatever your little heart desires! These treats are a great canvas to customize to your taste or surprise someone on a special occasion by adding one of their favorite ingredients.

Cherry Limeade Cobbler Bars

YIELD: 16 SQUARES

Sweet cherries and tart lime with irresistible buttery shortbread crust—and they're in bar form, convenient for a picnic or even a road trip! I love taking these to a summer gathering cut up into squares in a reusable container that doubles as a gift for the host. This way I'm left empty-handed and don't have to worry about forgetting the baking dish! Another plus to this being bars and not a traditional cobbler is that you can eat it with your hands.

Cooking spray

½ cup (112 g) vegan butter, melted

½ cup (100 g) organic cane sugar

1½ cups (188 g) all-purpose or gluten-free all-purpose flour

½ teaspoon baking soda

½ teaspoon baking powder

¼ teaspoon sea salt

1 bag (10 to 12 ounces [280 to 240 g]) frozen cherries, roughly chopped

Zest and juice of 1 lime

1 tablespoon (8 g) cornstarch

Preheat the oven to 375°F (190°C, or gas mark 5). Lightly grease an 8 × 8 inch (20 × 20 cm) baking dish with cooking spray.

In a bowl, cream together the butter and sugar.

Add the flour, baking soda, baking powder, and salt. Mix until well combined. Measure ¾ cup (175 ml) of the mixture from the bowl and set aside. Add the remainder of the mixture to the prepared baking dish and press firmly into the dish into a flat layer. Use the back of a spatula or your fingertips to really press it down into an even flat layer.

In the same bowl, mix in the cherries, lime zest, lime juice, and cornstarch until the cherries are evenly coated. Transfer to a baking dish and spread evenly over the layer of pressed crust.

Sprinkle the remaining crust mixture over the cherries and lightly pat it down so it sticks into the cherry filling. Bake for 45 minutes, until the top is golden. Cool completely before cutting. Putting it in the freezer for an hour will do the trick to rush things along, but I like to let them set overnight. Cut into 16 squares.

Note

For a shortcut, chop the cherries by adding them to the food processor and pulsing just a few times. If you don't have a hand zest or microplane, use the smallest grater section of a cheese grater to zest the lime.

Pumpkin Spice Affogato

YIELD: 4 SERVINGS

When leaves start falling, pumpkin becomes all the rage, along with pumpkin-spiced everything, the most notorious example being the pumpkin spice latte. But why have a latte when you can combine your caffeine intake with a spiced ice cream that actually has pumpkin in it?

1 can (13.5 ounces [380 ml]) full-fat coconut milk

1 cup (245 g) canned plain pureed pumpkin

½ cup (96 g) organic brown sugar

1 teaspoon vanilla extract

1 teaspoon ground cinnamon

½ teaspoon salt

¼ teaspoon ground cloves

¼ teaspoon ground ginger

⅛ teaspoon ground nutmeg

4 shots of brewed espresso

Place the coconut milk, pumpkin puree, brown sugar, vanilla, cinnamon, salt, cloves, ginger, and nutmeg into a blender and puree until completely smooth. Pour the mixture into an ice cream maker and churn for 25 minutes. Transfer the ice cream to the freezer.

Once firm enough to scoop, divide the ice cream among 4 bowls. Serve a shot of espresso with each one so that each person can pour the hot espresso over the ice cream and enjoy immediately.

DESSERTS

Banana Berry Cobbler

YIELD: 12 SERVINGS

Bananas add an unconventional spin on a timeless classic with this fruity cobbler. This texture of this dessert is similar to a coffee cake on the top but with a tantalizingly sweet baked fruit layer on the bottom.

½ cup (112 g) plus 2 tablespoons (28 g) nondairy margarine, divided

1 cup (130 g) sorghum flour

½ cup (79 g) brown rice flour

½ cup (65 g) tapioca starch

1 teaspoon xanthan gum

1 tablespoon (15 g) baking powder

1 teaspoon sea salt

¼ cup plus 2 tablespoons (90 g) packed brown sugar, divided

1 cup (235 ml) nondairy milk

1 teaspoon vanilla extract

3 or 4 bananas, sliced

2 cups (290 g) blueberries, raspberries, and/or blackberries

3 tablespoons (38 g) granulated sugar

2 teaspoons lemon juice

Preheat the oven to 350°F (180°C, or gas mark 4). Place the 2 tablespoons (28 g) margarine in an 11 × 7-inch (28 × 18 cm) baking dish. Place in the oven until the margarine melts. Remove the pan from the oven, tip to coat the bottom, and set aside.

In a large bowl, combine the sorghum flour, brown rice flour, tapioca starch, xanthan gum, baking powder, and salt. Using 2 butter knives or a pastry cutter, cut in the remaining ½ cup (112 g) margarine until small crumbs form. Stir in the ¼ cup (60 g) brown sugar until well mixed. Add the nondairy milk and vanilla extract, stirring until a thick batter forms.

In a separate bowl, toss together the sliced bananas and berries with the granulated sugar and lemon juice. Spoon the fruit into the baking dish over the melted margarine.

Drop the batter by the spoonful over the bananas and berries to mostly cover the fruit. Sprinkle with the remaining 2 tablespoons (30 g) brown sugar and bake for 45 minutes or until the fruit is bubbly and the top is golden brown. Let cool for about 15 minutes before serving.

PB and J Banana Muffins

YIELD: 12 MUFFINS

Everyone loves peanut butter and jelly! Paired with the perfectly baked goodness of a banana muffin, it's a delight for any age. Peanut butter and jelly isn't just for the kiddos! Depending on the size of your bananas, you may have more or less batter than needed, give or take a muffin or two. If you end up with a tiny bit more batter, divide it by the teaspoon onto the muffins ready to go in the oven!

¼ cup (60 ml) canola oil

½ cup (130 g) creamy peanut butter

1 cup (225 g) packed light brown sugar

½ teaspoon sea salt

1 teaspoon baking soda

2 teaspoons (10 ml) vanilla extract

2 ripe bananas, mashed

1½ cups (188 g) all-purpose or gluten-free all-purpose flour

1 tablespoon (15 g) roasted peanuts, crushed

¼ cup (60 ml) jelly of choice

Preheat the oven to 350°F (180°C, or gas mark 4). Line a 12-cavity muffin pan with cupcake liners.

Combine the canola oil and peanut butter in a bowl, and mix until smooth and creamy. Add the brown sugar and cream together with a spoon, hand mixer, or stand mixer. Add the salt, baking soda, vanilla, and mashed bananas. Mix until well combined. Add the flour and mix until well combined. Do not overmix.

Transfer ¼ cup (60 ml) of the batter to each liner of the prepared pan.

Bake for 15 minutes. Remove from the oven and add 1 teaspoon of jelly to each muffin top using a teaspoon. Create a small indent in the muffin when putting the jelly on top so it sets inside the muffin.

Return to the oven to bake for 18 to 20 minutes, until the top edges of the muffin have browned. Remove from the oven, and sprinkle ¼ teaspoon crushed peanuts over each muffin top. Sprinkle right onto the jelly so it sticks. Let cool completely.

Note

A stand or hand mixer is not necessary to cream sugar and butter. However, if using a spoon, sometimes it helps to press the soft butter into the sugar with the tines of a fork to break it up first and then cream with a spoon until fluffy and smooth. Easy peasy.

Crunchy PB Pretzel Chip Bites

YIELD: 16 BITES

I really like little portion-sized sweet treats. It helps me keep track of how many I eat so I can try to stop myself when I feel like I have had too many. For this one, I combined my favorite things: crunchy pretzel, smooth salty peanut butter, and melt-in-your-mouth chocolate chips. This is a super fun hands-on recipe for kids to make too! Pro tip on pretzel crushing: Add them to a blender or food processor and pulse until crumbs form. Or put the pretzels in a zip-seal bag and lightly smash them with a rolling pin or large end of a wine bottle until crumbs are formed.

½ cup (130 g) creamy peanut butter

3 tablespoons (60 g) maple syrup

¼ teaspoon sea salt

½ cup (118 g) crushed pretzels

2 tablespoons (30 g) oat flour

3 tablespoons (33 g) mini vegan chocolate chips

In a bowl, combine the peanut butter, maple syrup, and salt. Mix until smooth and creamy. Add ¼ cup (58 g) of the pretzel crumbs, oat flour, and chocolate chips. Mix until well combined. Scoop out 1 heaping teaspoon at a time and roll into balls. Set aside.

Put the remaining pretzel crumbs on a plate and roll each ball in the mixture until well coated.

Serve cold or at room temperature (I prefer cold). This will keep in an airtight container for up to 1 week in the refrigerator.

Note

If you don't have any oat flour, you can make your own oat flour by blending oats in a blender or food processor until a flour forms. Voilà!

Straightforward Strawberry Icebox Cake

YIELD: 4 PIECES

Icebox cakes are fun! This one goes a step further to utilize the latest on the market available in vegan whipped cream offerings. I've included options for the spray whip and whip available in the frozen section in the tub. My preference is always the tub version, but both work great! The spray can create roughly 2 cups (192 g) of whipped cream, exactly what this recipe calls for. You can also get the same amount from a tub. This recipe makes a smaller cake as this is best when enjoyed within three hours of making it and perfectly serves four people.

2 cups (192 g) vegan whipped cream

6 vegan rectangle-shaped graham crackers, 2 cut in half

1½ cups (220 g) strawberries, hulled and roughly chopped into small pieces

Add ½ cup (48 g) of whipped cream to a standard-size bread loaf pan. Spread into an even layer to create the base. Add the following layers.

Layer 1
Add 1 graham cracker plus half of a graham cracker to create 1 layer. The half of the graham cracker may overlap on the whole graham cracker slightly. Spread ¼ cup (24 g) of whip over the graham cracker, top with ½ cup (75 g) of strawberries, and spread an additional ¼ cup (24 g) of whip over the berries.

Layer 2
Add 1 graham cracker plus half of a graham cracker to create 1 layer. The half of the graham cracker may overlap on the whole graham cracker slightly. Spread ¼ cup (24 g) of whip over the graham cracker, top with ½ cup (75 g) of strawberries, and spread an additional ¼ cup (24 g) of whip over the berries.

Final Layer
Add 1 graham cracker plus a half a graham cracker, ½ cup (48 g) of whipped cream, and ½ cup (75 g) of strawberries. Crumble the remaining half graham cracker into tiny bits and sprinkle it over the top of the top.

Cover with plastic wrap and refrigerate for 1 hour. Cut into 4 slices and serve. Best if eaten within 3 hours.

Note

Swap out the strawberries for your berry of choice such as blueberries, raspberries, or blackberries, or combine them all for a berry icebox cake! I like to make this cake before I prepare dinner. By the time dinner has been served and eaten, the cake is the perfect texture as the graham cracker has softened into what resembles a cake.

No-Bake Berry Cheesecake

YIELD: 4 SERVINGS

Here is a cute dessert that has all the creaminess and tang of cheesecake, along with a juicy berry topping and a crunchy raw crust, without all the baking and waiting. These small, sweet bowls are definitely crowd-pleasers!

FOR THE CRUST MIX

¼ cup (36 g) raw almonds

¼ cup (45 g) Medjool dates, pitted

Pinch of salt

FOR THE CHEESECAKE FILLING

1½ cups (210 g) raw cashews, soaked in warm water for 30 minutes

½ cup (120 ml) water

¼ cup (60 g) plain coconut milk yogurt

3 tablespoons (45 ml) maple syrup

1 tablespoon (15 ml) lemon juice

Pinch of salt

FOR THE BERRY TOPPING

¾ cup (109 g) fresh blackberries

¾ cup (109 g) fresh blueberries

3 tablespoons (27 g) coconut sugar

2 tablespoons (28 ml) water

To make the crust

Place all the ingredients in a food processor and pulse until the mixture resembles coarse sand. Pour into a bowl and set aside.

To make the cheesecake filling

Drain and rinse the cashews. Place all the ingredients in a high-speed blender and puree until completely smooth. Chill in the refrigerator until ready to assemble.

To make the berry topping

In a small pan over medium heat, bring all the ingredients to a boil. Adjust the heat to medium-low and simmer for 7 to 10 minutes, stirring occasionally, until the berries have broken down and the mixture thickens.

Place 2 tablespoons (16 g) of the crust into the bottom of each small glass serving bowl. Push down gently on the crust to compact it. Next, carefully spoon 5 to 6 tablespoons (75 to 90 g) of the cheesecake filling into each bowl; tap down lightly to settle the filling.

You can chill the glasses for 10 minutes before completing the last step, but it's not necessary; it will just make the filling firmer for the topping to sit upon. Last, spoon 2 to 3 tablespoons (28 to 45 g) of berry topping into each glass. Chill for 30 minutes before serving.

Cookies 'n' Cream Dip

YIELD: 4 SERVINGS

Don't let savory dips and spreads have all the fun at your next party. Surprise people with this fluffy, sweet dip, and once the bowl is licked clean, shock the pants off them when you say that it is made with bean water!

FOR THE COOKIES

1½ teaspoons ground flaxseed

1 tablespoon (15 ml) hot water

¼ cup (48 g) plus 2 teaspoons organic cane sugar

¼ cup (56 g) coconut oil, at room temperature

1½ teaspoons unsweetened soy-free, nut-free nondairy milk

⅔ cup (83 g) unbleached all-purpose flour

⅓ cup (27 g) unsweetened cocoa powder

¼ teaspoon baking powder

Pinch of salt

FOR THE DIP

⅓ cup (80 ml) aquafaba (the liquid drained from a can of chickpeas)

1 cup (120 g) organic powdered sugar

¼ teaspoon cream of tartar

¼ teaspoon vanilla powder

Apple slices, for serving (optional)

To make the cookies

In a small bowl, stir together the flaxseed with the water and let set for 5 minutes. Using a stand or handheld electric mixer, whip the sugar and coconut oil on high speed until combined. Still mixing, add the flaxseed mixture and nondairy milk; beat until fluffy.

Sift the flour, cocoa powder, baking powder, and salt into a bowl. Add the dry mixture to the wet mixture and blend on medium speed until the cookie dough is crumbly but sticks together when pressed or squeezed. Form into a dough ball and refrigerate for 10 minutes.

Preheat the oven to 350°F (180°C, or gas mark 4) and line a large baking sheet with a silicone baking mat or parchment paper.

Lightly flour your workspace and rolling pin and roll out the cookie dough to ⅛ inch (3 mm) thick. Using a 2-inch (5 cm)-round cookie cutter, cut out the cookies and place on the baking sheet, repeating the process with the remaining dough.

Bake the cookies for 9 to 10 minutes or until firm. Transfer the cookies to a cooling rack. They will further harden as they cool.

To make the dip

Put the aquafaba in the bowl of a stand mixer fitted with the whisk attachment and beat the liquid on medium speed until foamy. Raise the speed to high and beat until the mixture has expanded considerably and peaks, about 15 to 20 minutes.

Slowly add the powdered sugar while the mixer is running as well as the cream of tartar and vanilla powder. Place half of the cookies in a food processor and pulse until crumbly. Carefully fold the cookies into the aquafaba fluff until combined and then transfer to a bowl and serve with the remaining cookies and apple slices for dipping. You can also store this dip in your refrigerator until ready to serve.

Chocolate Hazelnut Spread

YIELD: 20 SERVINGS

Inspired by Nutella, this vegan version leaves out the cow's milk and focuses on the delicious combination of roasted hazelnuts and rich chocolate with a hint of sweetness bringing it all together. This spread is a perfect topping for crackers or bread, or use it in place of other nut butters, such as peanut butter, in your favorite recipes.

2 cups (300 g) whole roasted hazelnuts, skinned

¼ cup (50 g) superfine granulated sugar

¼ cup (20 g) cocoa powder

¼ teaspoon sea salt

¼ cup (60 ml) or more nondairy milk

Combine the hazelnuts, sugar, cocoa powder, and salt in a food processor and blend until crumbly.

Slowly add the nondairy milk, about 1 tablespoon (15 ml) at a time, and blend until smooth. Depending on how dry your roasted hazelnuts are, you may need to add more or less nondairy milk than called for. I find that some of the hazelnuts I use require very little liquid to make a smooth spread, and some require a good bit of nondairy milk to even allow the mixture to blend properly.

Blend in the food processor until very smooth, about 5 minutes. Transfer to a sealed jar and store in the refrigerator up to 2 weeks.

Notes

To make superfine sugar, simply grind granulated sugar in a clean coffee or spice grinder until very fine.

If you cannot locate roasted, skinned hazelnuts, it's easy to make your own. Simply preheat your oven to 350°F (180°C, or gas mark 4) and spread the nuts on an ungreased baking sheet. Roast for about 10 minutes or until the skins begin to detach. Let the nuts cool and then transfer to a bowl or colander. Rub briefly with a clean kitchen towel until all skins have been removed.

Piña Colada Cupcakes

YIELD: 9 CUPCAKES

These cupcakes bring a taste of the Caribbean right to your very own kitchen with a pineapple cupcake base and an intensely flavorful coconut rum icing. Don't forget the cocktail umbrellas when serving.

FOR THE CUPCAKES

¾ cup (180 g) nondairy margarine, melted

1 cup (200 g) sugar

½ cup (80 g) crushed pineapple, well drained

1 teaspoon baking powder

½ teaspoon salt

1 cup (130 g) sorghum flour

½ cup (65 g) cornstarch

1 teaspoon xanthan gum

¼ cup (60 ml) light rum

¼ cup (60 ml) nondairy milk

3 tablespoons (45 ml) apple cider vinegar

FOR THE FROSTING

½ cup (95 g) coconut oil, at room temperature (firm)

2 tablespoons (30 g) nondairy margarine

2¼ cups (270 g) confectioners' sugar, divided

2 tablespoons (30 ml) pineapple juice (from canned pineapple above)

1 teaspoon rum extract

2 teaspoons coconut extract

To make the cupcakes

Preheat the oven to 350°F (180°C, or gas mark 4) and grease or line 9 cups of a standard-size cupcake pan.

In a large bowl, combine the melted margarine, sugar, and crushed pineapple. In a separate bowl, combine the baking powder, salt, sorghum flour, cornstarch, and xanthan gum.

In a small bowl, combine the rum and nondairy milk.

Gradually add the flour mixture to the margarine mixture about ¼ cup (30 g) at a time. After each addition of flour, add a little nondairy milk/rum mixture. Repeat until all the flour and liquid has been used. Mix vigorously until smooth. Add the vinegar 1 tablespoon (15 ml) at a time.

Divide the mixture among the cupcake liners and bake for 25 minutes or until a knife inserted into the middle comes out clean. Let cool completely on a wire rack before attempting to frost.

To make the frosting

In an electric mixer, combine the coconut oil, margarine, and 1 cup (120 g) of the confectioners' sugar and beat until smooth. Add 1 cup (120 g) more of the confectioners' sugar and then gradually add the pineapple juice, rum extract, and coconut extract and whip on the highest speed until fluffy. Add the remaining ¼ cup (30 g) confectioners' sugar and beat until stiff.

Using a pastry bag or a small plastic bag with a corner cut off, or with an offset spatula, pipe the frosting onto the cooled cupcakes and store in an airtight container in the refrigerator.

Chocolate Hazelnut Brownie Cheesecake

YIELD: 12 SERVINGS

This creamy dessert is frozen instead of baked and then thawed in the fridge to bring it to a cheesecake consistency. I recommend using an 8-inch (20.3 cm) springform pan for this. A bigger size can be used, but keep in mind that the smaller the pan, the taller your cheesecake.

FOR THE CRUST

1 cup (110 g) raw pecans

10 Medjool dates, pitted

½ cup (50 g) almond meal

½ cup (40 g) cocoa powder

FOR THE FILLING

3 cups (330 g) raw cashews, soaked in water to cover for at least 2 hours, then drained

1 cup (235 ml) coconut oil, melted

1 cup (235 ml) water

¾ cup (180 ml) agave nectar or maple syrup

1 cup (240 g) nondairy chocolate hazelnut spread, store-bought (such as Justin's brand) or homemade (page 213), plus more for garnish

1 teaspoon vanilla extract

To make the crust

In a food processor, combine the pecans and dates and pulse until uniform and crumbly. Transfer to a medium-size bowl. Add the almond meal and cocoa powder and stir to combine. Press the crust into the bottom of a springform pan.

To make the filling

In a food processor, blend together the soaked cashews, coconut oil, and water until very smooth, about 5 minutes. Add a touch more water if needed to get the cashews to blend well. Stir in the agave, 1 cup (240 g) chocolate hazelnut spread, and vanilla extract. Spread the filling evenly on top of the crust.

Cover tightly with aluminum foil and place in the freezer for 7 hours or overnight. Let thaw in the refrigerator for a couple of hours before serving. Garnish with a drizzle of melted chocolate hazelnut spread. Serve cold.

Dark Chocolate Chipotle Cake

YIELD: 10 SERVINGS

Spicy, sweet, and spongy, this dessert makes a nice alternative to plain ol' chocolate cake. Adjust the chipotle powder to your spiciness liking.

FOR THE CAKE

2 cups (400 g) sugar

1½ cups (350 g) nondairy margarine, melted

¾ cup (60 g) cocoa powder

1¼ cups (162 g) sorghum flour

½ cup (65 g) tapioca starch

½ cup (65 g) cornstarch

2 teaspoons xanthan gum

1 teaspoon salt

2 teaspoons baking powder

1½ teaspoons chipotle powder

1 cup (235 ml) nondairy milk

6 tablespoons (90 ml) apple cider vinegar

FOR THE CHOCOLATE GLAZE

1 cup (120 g) confectioners' sugar

¼ cup (60 ml) nondairy milk

½ cup (40 g) cocoa powder

2 tablespoons (28 g) nondairy margarine, softened

To make the cake

Preheat the oven to 350°F (180°C, or gas mark 4). Grease a standard-size Bundt pan well and lightly dust with cocoa powder.

In a large mixing bowl, combine the sugar, melted margarine, and cocoa powder.

In a separate bowl, combine the sorghum flour, tapioca starch, cornstarch, xanthan gum, salt, baking powder, and chipotle powder.

Alternate between adding the flour mixture and nondairy milk to the sugar mixture, scraping the sides as necessary. Once well mixed, stir in the vinegar 1 tablespoon (15 ml) at a time. Spread the cake batter evenly into the prepared pan.

Bake for 60 to 70 minutes or until a knife inserted near the middle comes out clean. Because Bundt cake pans vary, check after 55 minutes to make sure you don't end up with a burnt cake. Let cool completely on a wire rack.

To make the chocolate glaze

Mix all the ingredients together until super smooth. Make sure you wait until the cake is cool to make the glaze because it firms up quickly.

When your cake has thoroughly cooled, gently remove from the pan, place on a wire rack over a piece of waxed paper, and pour on the chocolate glaze. Let the glaze harden before transferring to a clean cake plate and slicing.

Pineapple Carrot Cake

YIELD: 16 SERVINGS

Carrot cake has always been one of my favorite special-occasion cakes, especially with pineapple added. The pineapple provides an extra dose of moisture while not competing with the flavor and texture of the carrots. Now we celebrate with this animal- and gluten-free version that is just as scrumptious as the original!

**FOR THE
DRY INGREDIENTS**

1¼ cups (162 g) sorghum flour

¾ cup (90 g) buckwheat flour

½ cup (65 g) potato starch

1 teaspoon xanthan gum

2 teaspoons baking soda

1 teaspoon baking powder

1 teaspoon sea salt

Dash of cardamom

1 teaspoon ground cinnamon

**FOR THE
WET INGREDIENTS**

1¾ cups (350 g) sugar

½ cup (112 g) nondairy margarine, melted

3 tablespoons (21 g) flaxseed meal mixed with 6 tablespoons (90 ml) warm water

1 teaspoon vanilla extract

2½ cups (375 g) peeled and shredded carrots

1 cup (165 g) crushed pineapple, drained

½ cup (75 g) applesauce

Preheat the oven to 350°F (180°C, or gas mark 4). Lightly grease and dust with sorghum flour two 9-inch (23 cm) cake pans or a 9 × 13-inch (23 × 33 cm) sheet cake pan.

To prepare the dry ingredients
Combine all the dry ingredients in a large bowl and mix well.

To prepare the wet ingredients
In a separate bowl, mix together all the wet ingredients until smooth. Add the wet ingredients to dry and mix thoroughly until you have a fairly thick batter.

Spoon the batter evenly between the 2 cake pans and bake on the middle rack of the oven for 30 minutes or until a knife inserted into the middle comes out clean. If using a sheet cake pan, bake about 5 minutes longer or again until a knife inserted into the middle comes out clean. Keep a watchful eye on your cake toward the last 5 minutes or so to check for doneness.

Let the cakes cool in the pans for about 20 minutes, and then invert the cakes onto cooling racks. Let cool completely before frosting.

Cream cheese frosting
Combine ½ cup (95 g) firm coconut oil, ½ cup (115 g) nondairy cream cheese, 4 to 5 cups (540 to 600 g) confectioners' sugar, plus 2 tablespoons (30 ml) almond milk into a bowl and beat with an electric mixer to make a quick and delicious frosting.

Mango Fritters
with Coconut Dipping Sauce

YIELD: 6 SERVINGS

You'll need a deep fryer for these or a skilled hand at deep-frying in a pot. If that's not too big of a concern, make these as soon as you can. You will not regret it.

PLANT-BASED SIMPLE

FOR THE FRITTERS

2 ripe mangoes

Vegetable oil, for frying

½ cup (88 g) yellow cornmeal

⅓ cup (42 g) plus ½ cup (65 g) potato starch, divided

½ cup (120 ml) almond milk

½ teaspoon sea salt

1 teaspoon ground cinnamon

Confectioners' sugar, for dusting

FOR THE DIPPING SAUCE

½ cup (120 ml) crème de coco

1 tablespoon (15 ml) lime juice

Zest of 1 small lime

To make the fritters

Peel and remove the pits from the mangoes. Slice the fruit into strips about 1 inch (2.5 cm) wide.

Pour the oil into a deep fryer to a depth of 5 inches (13 cm) and bring to 360°F (182°C).

Meanwhile, in a small bowl, whisk together the cornmeal, ⅓ cup (42 g) potato starch, almond milk, salt, and cinnamon to make a slightly thick batter. Spread the remaining ½ cup (65 g) potato starch on a plate.

Dredge each piece of mango in the potato starch and then immediately dip into the batter, covering completely. Hold over the bowl to allow extra batter to drip from the mango pieces. Be sure to dip each right before frying to make sure the batter goes into the fryer along with the mango.

Drop one by one into the hot oil and fry for 4 minutes or until golden brown. Remove from the hot oil with a skimmer and transfer to a paper bag or paper towels to drain. Repeat with the remaining fritters. Dust with the confectioners' sugar. Let cool.

To make the dipping sauce

Using an electric mixer or by hand, mix together the crème de coco, lime juice, and lime zest until fluffy.

Dip the fritters into the coconut sauce, take a bite, and fall back into complete mango ecstasy.

Note

Crème de coco is a mixture of coconut cream and sweetener used to make mixed drinks such as piña coladas. It can be found where mixed drinks fixings are sold. If you can't find it, use the thickest coconut cream you can find mixed with a little agave until sweetened.

Coconut Rice with Peaches and Rum Raisins

YIELD: 8 SERVINGS

This recipe is a more exotic take on the average rice pudding with its extra-creamy texture and sweet and tart flavors of fruit laced throughout. For a non-boozy option, soak the raisins in ½ cup (120 ml) pineapple juice mixed with 2 teaspoons rum extract.

½ cup (120 ml) light rum

1 cup (145 g) raisins

2 cups (390 g) uncooked jasmine rice

4 cups (940 ml) water

1 can (13.5 ounces [378 ml]) coconut milk

1 cup (200 g) sugar

Dash of salt, to taste (optional)

2 or 3 ripe peaches, chopped

Ground cinnamon, for sprinkling

The night before, combine the rum and raisins in a small bowl and cover. Let rest in the fridge overnight.

In a 1½-quart (1.4 L) saucepan over medium-high heat, add the rice, water, and coconut milk, stirring to combine. Bring the rice just to the beginning of a boil (not rolling) and then reduce the heat to low. Cover and let simmer until all the liquid has been absorbed and the rice is fluffy, 20 to 25 minutes. Do not stir the rice while it is cooking and avoid lifting the lid more than absolutely necessary.

Once the rice is fully cooked, stir in the sugar. Season lightly with salt.

In a small saucepan, stir together the peaches and rum raisins (including the liquid) and cook over medium heat, stirring occasionally, until the peaches are soft, about 2 minutes. Drain and gently stir the fruit into the rice.

Sprinkle with a touch of cinnamon. Serve hot or cold.

No-Churn Pineapple Basil Sorbet

YIELD: 8 SERVINGS

Pineapple and basil are a dream combo. Sweet and just a touch earthy with tropical notes. A fun variation on this recipe is to pour this mixture into popsicle molds! The faster you move from blending to freezer, the less icy the final sorbet will be. If you have xanthan gum in your arsenal of ingredients, you can always add ¼ teaspoon to the blender. This will aid maintaining a smooth mouthfeel and overall avoidance of an icy texture, but it's unnecessary. This is perfect for a summer day! If you have a blender that can't quite get this smooth, add 1 tablespoon (15 ml) of pineapple or orange juice as needed to get things moving.

1 bag (16 ounces [455 g]) frozen pineapple tidbits

1 can (20 ounces [567 g]) crushed pineapple, with juices

½ cup (120 ml) agave

¼ cup (10 g) packed fresh basil

Add the frozen pineapple, crushed pineapple and its juices, agave, and basil to a blender. Blend just long enough to reach a smooth consistency. Do not overblend as the frozen pineapple will begin to warm and the texture of the sorbet will get icier.

Transfer to a standard-size loaf pan, and press plastic wrap to the top of the mixture to push all the air out of the pan. Freeze overnight.

Note

If you wish to use 2 cups (330 g) of fresh pineapple in place of the frozen, you will need to use an ice cream maker. An ice cream maker will aerate the mixture and keep the ice crystals small so the texture does not get too icy.

Brittle Drizzle and Bananas with Coconut Ice Cream

YIELD: 4 SERVINGS

Ultra-luscious coconut ice cream covered in a sweet drizzle that turns crunchy and topped with caramelized bananas—is your mouth watering yet?

FOR THE COCONUT ICE CREAM

1 can (13.5 ounces [380 ml]) full-fat coconut milk

1 cup (60 g) unsweetened large coconut flakes

¼ cup (36 g) coconut sugar

1 teaspoon vanilla extract

¼ teaspoon salt

FOR THE CARAMELIZED BANANAS

2 teaspoons coconut oil

2 medium bananas, peeled and cut into ½-inch (6 mm) oval slices

2 tablespoons (24 g) organic brown sugar

⅛ teaspoon ground allspice, plus more for garnish

FOR THE BRITTLE DRIZZLE

6 tablespoons (90 ml) full-fat coconut milk

½ cup (96 g) organic sugar

1 teaspoon vanilla extract

⅛ teaspoon salt

To make the coconut ice cream
Place the coconut milk, coconut flakes, coconut sugar, vanilla, and salt in a blender and puree until completely smooth. Pour the mixture into an ice cream maker and churn for 25 minutes. Transfer the ice cream to the freezer.

To make the caramelized bananas
Heat the oil in a large skillet over medium heat. Add the bananas to the skillet and sprinkle the brown sugar and allspice over them. Cook for 3 to 4 minutes on each side until caramelized; adjust the heat to low to keep warm until ready to serve.

To make the brittle drizzle
In a large pan, stir the coconut milk, sugar, vanilla, and salt together over medium heat. Bring to a simmer, whisking occasionally, and cook until the mixture becomes smooth and tan in color and is pulling away from the edges of the pan to become a singular blob.

Divide the ice cream among 4 bowls, topping each one with caramelized bananas and the brittle drizzle. Add an extra shake of allspice and serve immediately.

Amaretto Cherry Ice Cream

YIELD: 6 SERVINGS

Booze plus dessert is one heavenly combination that is hard to mess up. But it is even easier to make right when the recipe includes beautiful dark, sweet cherries and an ultra-creamy ice cream.

FOR THE BOOZY CHERRY SAUCE

1 pound (455 g) dark sweet cherries, pitted

½ cup (115 ml) amaretto

2 tablespoons (24 g) organic brown sugar

FOR THE ICE CREAM BASE

1½ cups (210 g) raw cashews, soaked in warm water for 1 hour

1½ cups (355 ml) unsweetened plain soy milk

⅔ cup (103 g) dark sweet cherries, pitted

5 to 6 tablespoons (75 to 90 ml) maple syrup

2 to 3 teaspoons (10 to 15 ml) amaretto

⅛ teaspoon salt

Dark sweet cherries, pitted and chopped (optional)

To make the boozy cherry sauce

Place all the ingredients in a small pan over medium heat and bring to a simmer, uncovered. Adjust the heat to medium-low and simmer for 15 to 20 minutes, stirring occasionally. You want the cherries to be soft and breaking apart a bit. The sauce should coat a spoon once it has cooled slightly. Transfer the sauce to a small bowl and refrigerate.

To make the ice cream base

Drain and rinse the cashews. Place the soy milk and cashews in a high-speed blender and puree until completely smooth. Add the rest of the ice cream ingredients to the mixture and puree until smooth; you will see specks of cherry skins, which is fine.

To assemble

Pour the base into an ice cream maker and churn for 25 minutes or until thick but not frozen solid. In the meantime, prepare a 9 × 5 × 3-inch (23 × 13 × 7.5 cm) loaf pan by lining it with parchment paper.

When the ice cream base is ready, take the cherry sauce out of the refrigerator. Begin filling the loaf pan, alternating layers of the base and the cherry sauce and making 4 layers of the base and 3 thinner layers of sauce. Drag a butter knife through the mixtures to create swirls.

Place the ice cream in the freezer for 1 to 2 hours. When you are ready to serve, take the ice cream out and let soften for 5 to 10 minutes before scooping, if necessary. Garnish with fresh cherry pieces, if using, and serve in small bowls.

Note

If you do not have an ice cream maker, pour the base into a gallon (3.7 L)-size zip-top plastic bag, lay it flat, and freeze it until hard (about 1 hour). Then break it into smaller pieces and place the pieces into a food processor; process with an S-blade until smooth.

Dark Chocolate Orange Custard

This is ridiculously easy, ridiculously rich, and oh so good. This custard is dense and delicious and best reserved for an occasion when your taste buds deserve a little something special.

1 tablespoon (6 g) orange zest

1 teaspoon vanilla extract

1 bag (12 ounces [340 g]) nondairy chocolate chips

1 can (13.5 ounces [378 ml]) coconut milk

Mix together the orange zest, vanilla extract, and chocolate chips in a large heat-safe bowl.

In a small pan, over medium heat, bring the coconut milk to a boil. Pour the hot coconut milk over the chocolate chips and whisk together vigorously but carefully until smooth and uniform.

Transfer to 6 single-serving dishes, cover, and chill in the fridge until firm, at least 3 hours. This is best served cold.

Note

You can omit the orange zest and/or substitute vanilla extract with an equal amount of almond extract if you want to try different flavors.

DESSERTS

Almond Butter Cups

YIELD: 16 CANDIES

This recipe is slightly time-consuming, but that mostly lies in painting the cups with the melted chocolate; after that, it's smooth sailing. If you're a die-hard chocolate and almond fan like I am, these little treats are well worth the effort.

1 bag (12 ounces [340 g]) nondairy chocolate chips

1 cup (250 g) smooth or crunchy unsalted almond butter

1 teaspoon vanilla extract

2 tablespoons (15 g) confectioners' sugar

Dash or two of salt

2 tablespoons (30 ml) almond milk

Line about 16 mini muffin cups with mini muffin liners.

In a double boiler over medium-low heat, melt half of the chocolate until smooth.

Drop about 1 teaspoon of melted chocolate into each mini muffin liner and use the back of a spoon to smoosh the chocolate to coat the liners. Aim for making the chocolate about ⅛ inch (3 mm) thick. Chill the chocolate-coated liners in the freezer for about 10 minutes or until solid.

In the meantime, in a small bowl, mix together the almond butter, vanilla extract, confectioners' sugar, salt, and almond milk until smooth.

Once the chocolate shells are chilled, fill with the almond butter mixture, dividing evenly among all 16 cups. Chill again in the freezer while you melt the remaining chocolate.

In a double boiler over medium-low heat, melt the remaining half of the chocolate until smooth. Top the filled cups with a smooth layer of chocolate, spreading out to the edges of the paper lining, and chill once again in the freezer until firm, 5 to 10 minutes.

Store the cups in the fridge or freezer in an airtight container and serve chilled.

Mock Turtles

YIELD: 20 CANDIES

My dad loved "turtle" chocolate candies so much that it was an easy and always appreciated gift for him on any holiday. This is a healthier version of my dad's fave, with a very easy caramel made from Medjool dates.

20 Medjool dates, pitted

3 tablespoons (45 g) nondairy margarine

1 vanilla bean pod, split lengthwise and seeds scraped

40 whole pecan pieces

4 cups (700 g) nondairy chocolate chips

1 teaspoon coconut oil

In a food processor, combine the Medjool dates, margarine, and scraped vanilla seeds and pulse until uniformly sticky. Scoop out 1 to 2 teaspoons of the mixture, shape into a patty, and place 2 or 3 pecans on top. Flip over so that the pecans are on the bottom. Place on a baking sheet lined with a silicone mat or waxed paper. Repeat with the remaining date mixture and pecans to form 20 candies.

In a double boiler, melt the chocolate over medium-low heat. Stir in the coconut oil.

Dip just the bottoms of the candies into the chocolate to coat evenly and return to the baking sheet. Drizzle the tops with the remaining melted chocolate. Let harden in a cool place for at least 2 hours or until firm. Keep chilled to prevent melting.

Index